PINK FLOYD ARE FOGBOUND IN PARIS

Ben Graham

Other Books by Ben Graham

Music biography:
A Gathering Of Promises: The Battle For Texas's Psychedelic Music, From The 13th Floor Elevators To The Black Angels And Beyond (Zero Books)
Scatological Alchemy: A Gnostic Biography of The Butthole Surfers (Eleusinian Press)

Poetry:
For Everyone (The Winter Olympics)
Brighton Vortex
The Last Auk And Other Poems
Hard And Holy
Written In Mono
Shouting At The Sea (all Bleeding Cheek Press).

Fiction:
Nowhere To Go
We Are The Bad Rabbits And We Shall Overcome
Amorphous Albion (all Bleeding Cheek Press)

Pink Floyd Are Fogbound In Paris published by Bleeding Cheek Press, Brighton, August 2020

www.bleedingcheek.wordpress.com
bleedingcheekpress@gmail.com

Cover art & design © Daniel W J Mackenzie 2020, based on a photo by Gary Bodenham
dwj.mackenzie@gmail.com

PINK FLOYD ARE FOGBOUND IN PARIS

THE STORY OF THE 1970 KRUMLIN POP FESTIVAL

Ben Graham

FOREWORD BY BRIAN HIGHLEY

I left my hometown of Halifax more than forty years ago. I now have two grown-up daughters and a grown-up son, plus five grandchildren, all born in Devon or Somerset.

My first job away from Yorkshire was a managerial post at the Silver Blades ice rink in Bristol, where I often began work before dawn and didn't leave until after 2am due to a young Robin Cousins, who was training on my ice at crazy hours for the Olympics at which he won a gold medal. From Bristol I moved to Exeter, where I ran a club and promoted gigs including such diverse bands and solo artists as The Police, The Pretenders, Rick Wakeman, The Stranglers, Don McLean, Englebert Humperdinck, Stan Getz and many more. All successful sell-outs.

Even when I lived in Halifax I often wrote concert reviews for local newspapers and magazines. I continued this activity in Devon which eventually led to a completely new career as editor of a Devon newspaper. I also found time for a monthly feature in an international magazine and script writing for *The Two Ronnies*, Esther Rantzen and *Spitting Image*. (You'll find me on IMDB and Wikipedia)

Then along came *Trivial Pursuit*. I managed to bag the job of question writer thanks to my previous totally trivial career pattern. Initially this was part-time but soon developed into three or more editions each year, with associated media launches that found me opening an Oxford Street record store with the help of Sir Tim Rice, on stage at the London Palladium with Rik Mayall and Norman Wisdom, and riding down Regent Street with Linford Christie wrapping his legs around me on the pillion of a Harley-Davidson and the cast of *Starlight Express* as our roller-skating outriders. A knock-on from these events found me elected a Director of the British Comedy Society, attending presentations and award ceremonies and appearing on radio and TV chat shows and even enjoying a cameo role on *Last Of The Summer Wine*.

For 25 years I wrote all the UK *Trivial Pursuit* questions for the board games, the BBC TV show and three best-selling quiz books. My final games were for the US market: the Classic Rock Edition and the Rolling Stones Collectors Edition, for which my editor was former Stones bass guitarist Bill Wyman, and a Trivial Pursuit training game for KFC employees.

Despite all of the above, when I made a visit back to Halifax I walked into a Skircoat Green pub where I was instantly recognised as 'That bloke who ran the Krumlin Disaster.'

Three days in a field on the edge of the Pennines has obviously burnt (or should that be dripped?) its way not just into the psyche of the residents of Halifax, but also those much further afield. I've met people in New York, Toronto and Cairo who claimed they had been at Krumlin. One of my close neighbours in the small Devon village that is now my home swears he was there. Everyone has different memories. They all say it rained non-stop for three days and one even told me it snowed.

Of course they all claim to have watched Elton John. In his autobiography, *Me*, Elton refers to the cold, the wind and an unfinished stage. The stage was completed the Thursday before the festival was due to start and it was not raining when Elton appeared but, hey, why spoil a legend by telling the true story?

I'm delighted to say that is just what Ben Graham has tried to do in this book. He has done his research and will hopefully dispel some of the more creative Krumlin myths that have developed over the years.

Brian Highley

(Brian Highley's memoir, *In Pursuit Of Trivia*, includes his own personal view of the Krumlin Festival and a look at Halifax from the 1940s onwards. The book is internationally available in paperback and Kindle from Amazon.)

Brian Highley (foreground) and Derek McEwen, winter of 1969-70

The only festival in Britain to offer 50 hours of top bands

THE YORKSHIRE FOLK, BLUES & JAZZ FESTIVAL

Krumlin, Barkisland, Near Halifax, 14th, 15th and 16th August

150 acres of car park. 50-acre camp site. 300 toilets. ¼-acre of licensed bar, good, cheap food. Free covered accommodation. Beds for hire. All night concerts.

FRIDAY
(free to weekend ticket-holders)

PRETTY THINGS
JUICY LUCY.
ELTON JOHN.
GROUNDHOGS.
HUMBLEBUMS.
AND ALL NIGHT
FOLK, BLUES CONCERT.

SATURDAY

THE WHO.
MANFRED MANN CHAPT. III.
PENTANGLE.
FAIRPORT CONVENTION.
FOTHERINGAY.
GRAHAM BOND.
ALAN PRICE.
AMAZING BLONDEL.
RALPH McTELL.
CHAMP JACK DUPREE.
JO ANN KELLY
+ HEAVY FRIENDS
AND YET TO BE ANNOUNCED
BANDS.

SUNDAY

GINGER BAKER & AIRFORCE.
MUNGO JERRY.
TASTE.
EDGAR BROUGHTON.
YES.
QUINTESSENCE.
STEAMHAMMER.
MIKE WESTBROOK CONCERT
ORCHESTRA.
NATIONAL HEAD BAND WITH
THEIR HEAVY FRIENDS.
GREATEST SHOW ON EARTH.
JAN DUKES DE GREY WITH A 70-
PIECE CHOIR.

Post to NORTHERN ENTERTAINMENTS,
P.O. Box 5, Sowerby Bridge, Yorks.

ADDRESS ....

NAME ....

FULL WEEKEND .... SUNDAY ONLY ....

NO. OF TICKETS ....

P.O. VALUE ....

TICKETS BY CHEQUE/P.O./M.O. TO NORTHERN ENTERTAINMENTS.
FULL WEEKEND £2 10s. (£3 on day). SUNDAY ONLY £1 10s. (£2 on day)

PLEASE NOTE: £1 off weekend ticket

Offer closes first post Monday, 20/7/70. All orders for 30s. weekend
tickets will be returned after this date.

yorkshire folk, blues & jazz festival

8

PREFACE

When I was growing up in Sowerby Bridge in the 1970s and eighties, the Krumlin pop festival was a part of local mythology. It would be referred to knowingly whenever the subject of classic rock bands or the "hippy era" in Calderdale came up in conversation. No-one seemed to know who had played at it — names including Jimi Hendrix and The Rolling Stones would be assertively contributed, then tentatively dismissed by others — but everyone knew it had been a complete disaster. Rain had done more than stop play: in the eyes of some, it had conclusively proved the folly of trying to put on any kind of counter-cultural event in this proudly conservative corner of West Yorkshire. The story of Krumlin was in grave danger of having a spurious moral attached to it, and of being held up as a prime example of exactly why "the sixties" were always doomed to failure.

In fact, Halifax and the surrounding valleys of the Calder, Ryburn and Hebble had a thriving artistic underground that blossomed during the late sixties and survived through the 1970s and beyond. It was more obvious in some corners than in others, and by the time I was young it was conceded that nearby Hebden Bridge had indeed fallen to the hippy incomers, with their foolish notions of organic health food, meditation, yoga, worker's cooperatives, consciousness raising and communal living.

Just a few months before Krumlin, the A-Wake Festival of May 1970 saw the young, turned-on, creative free spirits who had moved to Hebden over the previous few years really make their mark for the first time, with a combination of music, art and street theatre that bewildered and enchanted in equal measure. This set the groundwork for the still-thriving Hebden Bridge Arts Festival, and began the rebirth of this sleepy, then-declining market town into one of the most desirable places to live in the UK (devastating floods notwithstanding).

Hebden was not unique however. Other towns in the area, including Sowerby Bridge and Halifax, also attracted artists, writers, musicians and visionaries attuned to the more adventurous spirit of the times. Many had studied art at one of the universities in Leeds or Bradford, where the lecturers included the poet, painter and provocateur Jeff Nuttall. Attracted by cheap house prices, the availability of derelict mills and warehouses for studio space, and the inspiring possibilities of the stunning moorland landscape, many stayed, and for a time the region was known as the Yorkshire Vortex for its ability to draw in some of the most interesting artists of the day.

Radical theatre groups prospered in particular, including John Bull Puncture Repair Kit, led by Al Beach and Mick Banks, who also founded the Halifax Arts Lab, AKA Northern Open Workshops (NOW). Equally notable was Welfare State, based in Leeds, Bradford and Burnley. In 1976, former members of Welfare State founded the Independent Outlaw's University that evolved into IOU Theatre, now highly successful and still based in Halifax at the Dean Clough Arts Complex.

The region was also well-served for live music. Calderdale, Huddersfield and the area stretching from Halifax to Bradford were something of an epicentre for the 1960s folk revival, with now-legendary figures like John Martyn, Martin Carthy and The Watersons often performing at small pub venues alongside traditional singers and musicians. It's notable that Christy Moore, the greatest living Irish folk singer, songwriter and musician, initially made his name performing in pubs in Halifax, where he lived for a time. As we shall see, the Krumlin Festival drew strongly from this fertile local folk circuit.

Throughout the sixties, Halifax was also home to the jazz club Plebeians (known as Plebs). While in the first half of the decade it featured the likes of Humphrey Lyttleton and Acker Bilk, by 1965 it was playing host to Rod Stewart and London mod legends The Action. The Graham Bond Organisation, Joe Cocker, Chris Farlowe's Thunderbirds, The Koobas, Jimmy Cliff, The Skatalites and Steam Packet (featuring Brian Auger and Julie Driscoll), were some of the other names to appear at Plebs, alongside DJ-led northern soul all-nighters considered some of the best in the country, before the club closed its doors for good in May 1968.

Local celebrity wrestler Shirley Crabtree, better known as Big Daddy, opened his own club in Halifax in 1963, alongside his manager brother Max. They put on big-name pop acts including The Kinks and Donovan. In 1967 Plebs' founder Paul Mountain took over the lease on the Crabtree brothers' club and turned it into Clarence's, which became the centre of the Halifax music scene throughout the seventies.

Barclay James Harvest, Supertramp, Roxy Music, Thin Lizzy, Dr Feelgood and Kilburn & The High Roads (featuring Ian Dury) all played at Clarence's during the first half of the decade. At the end of 1976 it was renamed The Good Mood and booked a credible selection of punk and post-punk acts over the next few years, including Generation X (with Billy Idol), The Saints, The Only Ones, Big in Japan (featuring Holly Johnson, Bill Drummond and Ian Broudie), Joy Division, Wire, The Cure and Dexy's Midnight Runners.

Sadly, by the mid-eighties, when I started going out in Halifax as a teenager, the local music scene was virtually moribund. Despite occasional gigs by indie bands like Pulp or The Wedding Present, who would go on to greater success in the nineties, and a quirky DIY movement of local bands driven by boredom and desperation, Halifax felt like the archetypal forgotten town where nothing ever happens — which made the stories of the Krumlin Festival all the more fascinating.

Returning to live in Halifax after attending college in London, I started performing at weekly poetry nights held at the Puzzle Hall Inn in Sowerby Bridge, back when the landlord was the eccentric and much-missed Jerry Melanie. The back corridor leading to the toilets was wallpapered with newspaper cuttings, mainly from the Halifax *Evening Courier,* that told the story of Krumlin as it happened. Many an evening I stood with a pint of Taylor's, trying to read those faded articles between poetry sets, and wondering if the full story of the festival would ever be uncovered. It wasn't until I'd left Halifax again, moving to Brighton in 1997, that I finally decided to uncover the story for myself.

I'm indebted to those researchers who went before me, particularly John S. Wharton, whose work kept interest in the Krumlin story alive for many years. Indeed, it was the expectation that John would publish his own account of the festival that caused me to put aside this book for around eight years or more. I returned to it at the end of 2019, when it suddenly struck me that the 50th anniversary of Krumlin was fast approaching, in August 2020, and that in terms of getting the work I'd already done into the public eye it was surely now or never.

In the intervening years I had myself become involved in organising a three-day music festival in Yorkshire, with little prior experience and far more enthusiasm than money or resources. Festival 23, which took place near Sheffield in the summer of 2016, was a far smaller affair than Krumlin, catering to a mere 500 people rather than 25,000, and the logistics of putting on big outdoor events are very different now to what they were in 1970. Nevertheless it was a steep learning curve, and going back to the Krumlin story after having similarly run an outdoor camping and music fest, on a shoestring with a tiny crew of valued co-conspirators, I felt a great deal more empathy with what Brian Highley and the late Derek McEwen went through.

Re-reading my manuscript and going back to my sources to prepare a second draft, there were many moments of "there but for the grace of god went I". At Festival 23 we were extremely lucky with the weather, and I'm acutely aware that if it had rained heavily our event would have been very differently received. At Krumlin, of course, they were not so lucky.

Fifty years on, it's possible to see the humorous side of the Krumlin debacle. Sometimes the story reads like a cross between *Withnail & I* and *Last Of The Summer Wine,* and I've tried to capture that. But it's not just the story of a disaster: it's the story of what could have been. In recent years, Halifax, Hebden Bridge and Todmorden have once more become focal points for exciting live music, as well as art, theatre, literature, film and TV. The fact that artists, writers and musicians are once again being drawn towards the Calder Valley casts the Krumlin Festival in a welcome new light.

In the dark days of the 1980s and nineties, when Halifax and Calderdale felt like the land that time forgot, Krumlin was held up as an example of risible hubris. It supposedly proved that trying to make anything like that happen round here was doomed to failure, and in that respect it perhaps acted as an unconscious dampener on all of our efforts to form bands, write books, put on gigs and generally make our mark. It felt as though coming from Halifax (or Sowerby Bridge) would always be seen as a bit of a joke, and that was certainly one of the reasons why I eventually left.

I'm happy to say that this is no longer the case. With Halifax and Calderdale now celebrating its rock music heritage rather than disparaging it, the time has come for the Yorkshire Folk, Blues and Jazz Festival at Krumlin to be re-assessed. It now seems less like a dated folly and more like a brave, if doomed, foreshadowing of the region's current renaissance. It becomes a key part of an ongoing musical history of the area, an example of how, way back in 1970, there were already people struggling against the odds to *do something,* and it very nearly came off.

In the mid-nineties I wrote and edited a short-lived music fanzine in Halifax called *News From Nowhere.* Its title reflected the way many of us felt about the town then, as well as the characteristic self-deprecating humour of the region. This was the beginning of what has become a career of sorts in music journalism, with my work appearing in publications including *The Fly, Stool Pigeon, The Quietus* and *Shindig!*

I've also written two volumes of music biography, *A Gathering Of Promises: The Battle for Texas's Psychedelic Music, From The 13th Floor Elevators To The Black Angels And Beyond* (Zero Books, 2015) and *Scatological Alchemy: A Gnostic Biography Of The Butthole Surfers* (Eleusinian Press, 2018). Both of those books covered American music; although I published an autobiographical novel set in Halifax, *We Are The Bad Rabbits And We Shall Overcome* (Bleeding Cheek Press, 2011), this is the first time I've written about the music history of the place I grew up in.

It is a story I've long wanted to write. It's a labour of love, dedicated to my original hometown and all of its contradictory, frustrating, eccentric and amusing ways. For better or worse, Halifax made me; and for me, the Krumlin story in many ways captures the essence of what Halifax is all about.

This short book also allows me to indulge my love of 1960s and seventies music and culture, reflecting an abiding fascination with the party that seemingly ended just before I was born. Obviously I was not there myself, and I've not tried to do many interviews with people who attended the festival, if only because memory is a vague, subjective thing, and everyone has their own version of who played and what happened when.

Unless otherwise credited, the extended quotes in italics (and a few others) were taken from the excellent UK Rock Festivals website. I have also relied on contemporary press cuttings, mostly from the Halifax *Evening Courier,* in putting together the story. The report of the Rochdale Civil Aid group on their role in the festival was essential, and often unintentionally hilarious. My final primary source was Brian Highley's own account in his book *In Pursuit Of Trivia,* and Brian's own comments on the first draft of my manuscript.

I've tried to paint an honest picture of the run-up, events and aftermath of the festival. At the same time, and contrary to what Brian says in his foreword, I hope I haven't dispelled all of the myths that have grown up around Krumlin. It was, after all, the myth that attracted me, and as a former journalist and tall tale-teller himself, I'm sure Brian would agree that sometimes you have to "print the legend". Hopefully, with *Pink Floyd Are Fogbound In Paris,* I've got the balance right.

Shelter From The Storm

Gary Bodenham: "Determined to stick it out, I glugged more cider as the rain sheeted down. At some point a stream of water trickled into my plastic bag and was gradually soaked up by my greatcoat. By midnight I was a shivering drunken wreck, aware only of the sound of the rain on plastic and Sandy Denny's beautiful voice echoing around the moors as Fotheringay bravely battled with the elements.

"I realised I had to move or I would die. I staggered to our tent, to the fantastic news that there was a spare DRY sleeping bag. Discarding my wet clothes and getting into the sleeping bag was like sinking into warm cotton wool, and I slept the sleep of angels. In the morning we woke to devastation, it was all over, and apparently fans were being treated for exposure. As I walked up the road home with a muddy blanket over my shoulders I felt like a survivor from the Somme."

Dennis Poole: "We avoided the fuzz and spent the evening before the storm drinking a gallon of beer each and smoking dope. I remember lying on my back looking at the stars and grabbing hold of clumps of earth because I thought I was going to take off. It was just as well we were out of it because when we woke up the next day the stage had mostly blown away, the crowd had split and we were left with the task of trying to get home.

"What I can't mention is the state of the 'facilities'. Perhaps I should. They were basically a set of oil drums cut down in large tents. The choice was not Ladies or Gents (they were unisex), the choice was top of the hill or bottom. I will leave to your imagination which one was best."

Stewart Wainfor: "Due to the mixture of alcohol and stuff, I don't really recall much until I woke with my head outside the tent, which was flapping madly in the wind, with only one pole standing. After extracting myself from the remains of the tent and my sleeping bag and trying to stand up in a Force 10 gale, I looked at the scene of total destruction - it looked like the corporation rubbish tip."

"For two of the three summers worked on this contract the Pennines were lashed by some of the heaviest rain on record, with 66 inches falling during the first year, twice the national average, and as much as 4 inches in 2

days on at least one occasion. Moreover, the cloud here is often down to around 1000 feet, and much of the site was frequently lost in cloud which at times reduced visibility to nil" – from a report on the construction of the nearby Scammonden Dam section of the M62 motorway, 1969-1971.

On the weekend of August 14-16, 1970, roughly 25,000 people gathered in a field in Krumlin, Barkisland, for the first Yorkshire Folk, Blues and Jazz Festival. It was also the last. The programme promised headlining sets by The Who, Pink Floyd and Ginger Baker's New Air Force, the latter to feature a secret special guest rumoured to be either Jimi Hendrix or Peter Green.

In fact, many of the advertised performers didn't get to play at all, and by the third morning the festival site was officially declared a disaster area. Although it was midsummer, temperatures had dropped to less than four degrees Celsius, and felt much colder due to gale force winds and heavy rain turning to hail and sleet, on a bleak and unprotected hillside high on the Yorkshire moors. On Saturday night, most of those remaining sought shelter in the beer tent, which collapsed as the central pole snapped under the force of the winds.

Miraculously, and contrary to press reports at the time, no-one was killed, although hundreds of people were treated for exposure after ambulances struggled to reach the site. Tents were ripped from their moorings and never seen again. The stage was flooded and the festival was cut abruptly short on Saturday night, with headline bands unable to play.

Rip-offs and fraud were rife all down the line, with the two inexperienced promoters suffering the worst of it. One disappeared on Friday night and was thought to be wandering the wind and rain-swept moors after some kind of nervous breakdown, while his partner was left to try to hold together the rapidly unravelling festival virtually single-handed. What started out as a wild creative adventure, fuelled equally by an entrepreneurial eye for the main chance and a genuine desire to bring the musical and artistic culture of the times to a then-overlooked corner of West Yorkshire, soon turned into a nightmare of financial chaos, bitter accusations and bankruptcy.

At the time, the Krumlin Festival was the worst disaster in British rock festival history. It remains obscure, yet still lingers on the fringes of our collective memory, like Banquo's Ghost haunting the ongoing banquet of corporate-sponsored, big money music festivals that continue to proliferate each summer. As late as 2008, the tale of Fairport's Dave Pegg soiling himself onstage at Krumlin was mentioned in the *Observer* newspaper at number seven in a list of "Most Memorable Festival Moments".

Yet in 1970, the rock festival scene was still in its infancy. A month after this debacle, at the other end of the country, a young farmer named Michael Eavis held the very first Glastonbury Fayre at Worthy Farm in Pilton. This would of course evolve into the Glastonbury Festival of today, the undisputed flagship event of the global music festival circuit. But for freak weather conditions, could things have been very different, and the Krumlin Festival become the internationally famous and enduring annual extravaganza, with Glastonbury consigned to the role of inglorious footnote in rock history?

Probably not; but Krumlin is worth remembering for reasons other than bad weather and poor organisation. The line-up is arguably more attractive now than it would have been at the time, as second-tier acts from that era have gained a sizable, appreciative cult following as the decades have passed. Around 1970 many of the acts that started out in the sixties were creating some of their most interesting work, before they either went into a decline, called it a day, or achieved greater commercial success while making far less adventurous music. Even taking into account cancellations and no-shows, Krumlin featured a bill of fare that today looks decidedly impressive.

Most famously, Elton John played his first UK festival appearance, and his last British show as a relative unknown, on Friday night at Krumlin, immediately prior to the US tour that made him a global superstar. His stunning set is remembered as the highlight of the festival, but the Krumlin line-up is also particularly appealing for fans of the psych-tinged folk-rock that reached a creative zenith during this period. Just seeing Sandy Denny's Fotheringay, Pentangle at their peak and *Full House* era Fairport Convention on the same bill now seems like a dream. There was also a pronounced leaning towards progressive jazz-rock, in the shape of Graham Bond (in his *Holy Magick* phase), Ginger Baker's Air Force, Mike Westbrook and Manfred Mann Chapter III, among others. Heavy acid-rockers The Groundhogs and The Pretty Things performed at their creative, experimental peak, and the folk programme featured a long list of brilliant acoustic singer-songwriters. Looked at today, it all adds up to a boutique, leftfield line-up seemingly curated with today's vintage music aficionado squarely in mind.

The 'disaster' tag must also be put into perspective. Sadly the last twenty years have seen far worse festival tragedies than Krumlin, with numerous deaths at major music events around the world due to extreme weather, crush conditions, drugs, violence and even terrorist attacks. In May 2017, the Guardian published "From Altamont to Fyre: A History of the Worst Music Festival Disasters." Unlike the more light-hearted *Observer* piece of nine years earlier, it made for grim reading, and Krumlin didn't even get a look-in.

In this context, the Yorkshire Folk, Blues and Jazz Festival plays out less like a genuine tragedy, and more like a black comedy. Fifty years after it took place, Krumlin would be on any hipster time traveller's festival bucket list. Just wrap up warm, and don't forget to bring your space-age waterproofs.

Back To The Garden

It's easy to forget, now that music festivals are a safe, familiar fixture of the Great British Summertime, the utopian premise upon which their forebears were founded, and the degree to which this premise was widely believed in and taken to heart. While most were just looking for sex, drugs and rock n' roll, a small but passionate number of young hippy festival-goers in the late 1960s and early seventies believed fiercely in the scene's mythology — the promise of some kind of revolutionary, millennial arcadia just around the corner, the much-trumpeted coming of the Age of Aquarius — with a messianic fervour that invites comparison with the religious cults and movements of the Middle Ages.

Many who boarded the ferry to the Isle of Wight, for instance, for the second of the three iconic festivals that took place there (before the event's corporate, retro-tinged revival in the 2000s), genuinely thought that this windswept, conservative rural holiday resort could be their Promised Land. They nurtured the notion that they could stay and somehow convert it into a kind of offshore freak reservation, an Isle of Avalon reborn, away from the oppression and industrialism of mainland Britain. Their testimonies seem laughable now, quaint and almost unbelievable; but there's a great sadness in looking back, too. Even for those of us not yet born at the time, it's like looking back to our own childhood, and an innocent faith and optimism that we've long since irrevocably lost.

Jazz and folk festivals had been reasonably commonplace occurrences throughout the 1950s and early sixties: staid, one-day events featuring the likes of George Melly, Ted Heath and Johnny Dankworth. By 1959 they were starting to attract what *Melody Maker* termed "the weirdies" — youthful beatniks and CND supporters in beards and duffel coats, and the furtive, sharp-dressed, pill-popping mods of MacInnes' *Absolute Beginners*. It was inevitable, as home-grown rock music grew in stature with the next decade, that the aggressive young electric bands would begin to infiltrate this scene.

The Rolling Stones played the Richmond Jazz Festival for the first time in 1963, and headlined the following year. In 1965 they were joined by The Yardbirds and Manfred Mann, and in consequence outraged locals forced the festival's move to Windsor, where in 1966 The Who incited the audience to join them in acts of auto-destruction, while Eric Clapton, The Spencer Davis Group and The Small Faces brought up the rear.

Even in the so-called Summer of Love however, the number of outdoor rock festivals could easily be counted on one hand. In 1967 Windsor played host to The Small Faces, Donovan, The Nice and Ten Years After, while the unbearably twee-sounding Festival of the Flower Children at Woburn Abbey boasted The Bee Gees, Marmalade, "firework displays and free flowers and sparklers." 1968 saw Pink Floyd play the first free concert in Hyde Park, and also the first Isle of Wight Festival, AKA "The Great South Coast Bank Holiday Pop Festivity." This was actually a pretty low-key, one-day fundraising event for a new municipal baths in the tiny village of Godshill, albeit one supported by Jefferson Airplane, The Crazy World of Arthur Brown, Fairport Convention, The Move, Tyrannosaurus Rex, The Pretty Things and compere John Peel.

In 1969 both Blind Faith and The Rolling Stones staged free concerts in Hyde Park. Fleetwood Mac, John Mayall, Ten Years After and Led Zeppelin performed at the Bath Blues Festival to an audience of 30,000, including one Michael Eavis, who with his wife Jean had broken in through the fence without paying and was inspired to start planning his own similar event, while also inadvertently pioneering the traditional method of free entry to said event for decades to come. Across the Atlantic, Woodstock stumbled starry-eyed and stoned into the history books, but the only British event to even come close to its stature was the second Isle of Wight Festival the following week, with 200,000 attendees to Woodstock's 400,000, and acts including Dylan, The Who, The Moody Blues, Free, The Nice and Joe Cocker.

In 1970 the second Bath Blues Festival featured Led Zeppelin, The Byrds, The Mothers of Invention, Jefferson

Airplane and others. The underground free festival circuit was also starting to get off the ground, and generally involved Hawkwind and The Pink Fairies setting up under polythene in a muddy field somewhere. A notable early event (not originally intended to be free) was Mick Farren's Phun City, at which Detroit's proto-punk rock revolutionaries The MC5 kicked out the jams in sedate Worthing, ably assisted by the aforementioned Pink Fairies, The Pretty Things, Kevin Ayers and even William Burroughs (but not Free, who were booked, but refused to live up to their name and demanded payment that was not forthcoming).

And then there was Krumlin. It's tempting to imagine the naive, idealistic hippies who glimpsed a vision of Avalon on the Isle of Wight the year before hitching up to Yorkshire still fired by the same spirit, only to have it crushed and blasted out of them by the three days that followed. We can conjecture how this might have left them cynical, tubercular and hollow-eyed, already plotting the punk counter-revolution that lay six years in the future; that would characterise the colder, harder decade that had just begun. Was Krumlin in fact where the tide turned? Where the sixties dream washed up, hit the impermeable northern slopes and began its retreat, even as, in the south, the party still continued for a few more months? Perhaps: with apologies to Hunter S. Thompson, they say that if you look closely at a certain Barkisland hillside, you can still see the tidemark.

Wolf Country Blues

The Reverend John Watson was the area's first local historian during the mid-eighteenth century. Ordained in 1749, he was Curate of Halifax from 1750-1754, and Curate of Ripponden from 1754-1766. In 1759 he was elected a fellow of the Society of Antiquaries in London, and his publications included *Survey Of A House In The Back Lane Of Halifax, History And Antiquities Of The Parish Of Halifax In Yorkshire,* and *Druidical Remains In Or Near The Parish Of Halifax In Yorkshire.*

In the latter volume, Watson described a stone circle called a "wolf fold," which he associated with druidic practices. Found in Barkisland, the circle was about 100ft across and comprised an elliptical arrangement of stones. In 1905, five sets of cremated remains and an urn were reported to have been found within a small mound at the centre of the circle.

Watson claimed that the name Barkisland meant 'Birch Tree Country,' but it has also been translated as meaning 'Wolf Country.' Mesolithic and Bronze Age artefacts have been found near the suggestively-named Ringstone Reservoir, and a modest stone circle, as well as possible mounds and earthworks, can be seen nearby. There are also stories of stone circles being submerged beneath the reservoir, built in 1886 by Thomas Hawsley. The reservoir itself covers 49 acres, holds 245 million gallons, and is sixty feet deep.

A few miles east, nestling in the hills overlooking the River Ryburn as it flows into Sowerby Bridge, there to join with the Calder, is the tiny village of Mill Bank. Like nearby Hebden Bridge, Mill Bank was all but derelict and abandoned by the early sixties, until an influx of out-of-towners — loosely bohemian, young refugees from the urban diaspora— began buying up run-down farmhouses and terraces for next to nothing, starting their own commuter community away from what was then, in the days before Thatcherite survivalism, widely termed the rat race.

In 1969 the new landlord of the Anchor Inn in Mill Bank was a 25-year-old former schoolteacher named Brian Highley.

Among the regulars were 30-year-old Derek McEwen, a local folk music promoter and advertising salesman for the Halifax *Evening Courier*, and Alan Jones, who worked in the *Courier*'s art department.

Highley had a flair for publicity and had some experience promoting college events in his student years. The son of a local dance band leader, he had grown up around the last days of music hall and felt that showbiz was in his blood. McEwen meanwhile was at the time sharing a flat with the Irish Folk Singer Christy Moore, then just at the beginning of a tumultuous career that would eventually lead to him becoming one of the most famous, respected and controversial figures in traditional music.

Moore recalled his first meeting with McEwen in his autobiography *One Voice: My Life in Song* (Hodder & Stoughton, 2003). The singer had travelled from Ireland to Manchester and was working the folk club circuit there when McEwen ("a quietly spoken Mancunian from Chadderton") approached him after a gig at the Kingsway Hotel near Rochdale in 1967.

"He offered me a deal," Moore wrote. "I would move into his place in Rochdale where he ran a fish and veggie shop on Oldham Road. He gave me a three-sided bedroom and I drove a greengrocer's van round the estates of East Manchester. He also became my agent and friend and we lived a shambolic life together for two years."

Derek introduced Christy to many new artists and songs through his eclectic record collection, including the works of the great patriarch of northern English folk, Ewan McColl, and they would spend their nights at the local folk clubs, attempting to get Christy bookings and to pick up women. But after three months, Christy recalled, "the bottom fell out of the vegetable van and we moved over the Pennines to Halifax. We travelled by night at speed."

Derek by this time had married (with Christy acting as best man), and so Christy moved alone into a damp and run-down stone cottage at Syke Lane, Causeway Foot near Bradshaw, on the outskirts of Halifax. From here he worked a circuit that included Sunday nights at the Bradshaw Tavern, the Topic

Club in Bradford, the Upper George in Halifax, the Anchor in Brighouse and the moveable feast that was Richard Collins' Grass Roots Club. McEwen's marriage soon foundered and when, in 1969, Moore was re-housed by the council, on the basis that his cottage was unfit for human habitation, McEwen followed him to a two-bedroom flat in one of the newly-built tower blocks in Mixenden.

At 83 Jumples Court, Moore and McEwen played host to a constant stream of touring folk musicians, raucous all-night jam sessions, and unannounced visits from the local flying squad, who were convinced that the flat was the base of an IRA terrorist cell. As well as being Moore's informal booking agent, McEwen loosely represented fellow Irish folk musicians Dave Shannon and Sam Bracken, and such singers as Gillian McPherson, Roger Sutcliffe, Martin Wyndham-Read and Dave Burland, any number of whom might be found dossing down at Jumples Court on any given night.

In September 1969 McEwen started his own folk night at the Grove pub in Brearley, between Luddenden Foot and Mytholmroyd. Folk at the Grove's first evening featured Christy Moore, Dave Burland and Roger Sutcliffe, but despite this auspicious start barely lasted the year. Moore was ready to move on, having already recorded his debut album, *Paddy on the Road*, in London with Dominic Behan. Brian Highley's suggestion of using a photo of Christy posing on the unfinished M62 motorway for the cover was abandoned in favour of a more conventional portrait of the singer sat under a tree, his guitar case by his side.

Christy Moore on the M62: the rejected potential cover photo for Paddy on The Road.

A Northern Entertainment

Brian Highley had started his own successful folk nights at the Anchor in Mill Bank, with Christy Moore, Hamish Imlach and Mike Harding among the regular performers. It was late '69, and Woodstock was in the news: the idea of staging a summer folk festival seemed a natural one, and indeed the Anchor overlooked an idyllic rolling field that seemed more than suitable. Alas, the farmer who owned the land disagreed, and refused to let it be trampled on by the hordes of long-haired, flower-power hippies he imagined descending en mass on his property.

At this point Alan Jones made his excuses and left, but Highley and McEwen, their pride hurt by the farmer's rude refusal, vowed to press on. In fact, they decided that they would organise a far bigger festival than the one originally envisaged. McEwen got the *Courier* to run a story announcing that the pair were looking for a large field suitable for a "colossal" event.

A few farmers came forward offering their land, but Neil 'Pop' Hirst was the only one who didn't ask for payment upfront. Moreover his 40-acre site at Krumlin, Barkisland, formed a natural amphitheatre and was in some ways ideally placed, high on the Pennine hills and close to the Yorkshire-Lancashire border. Manchester, Leeds, Bradford, Huddersfield, Halifax and many other northern towns were all within easy travelling distance.

Highley and McEwen did some quick maths on the back of an envelope and concluded that, with a catchment area of some 40 million people, they could draw up to 150,000 music fans to Hirst's Banquet House Farm, despite the fact that the site could only be reached via steep, single-lane roads. As a result, their plans grew more ambitious.

Why stop at folk? Why not blues, why not jazz? Why not bring some big-name rock bands to this isolated, overlooked corner of Yorkshire? Why shouldn't Krumlin be the Woodstock of Northern England? After all, that too was an obscure rural backwater, home to a handful of bohemians and folk musicians, until the festival put it on the map. Highley and McEwen registered themselves as Northern Entertainments, of PO box 5, Sowerby Bridge, and began laying the groundwork for the first Yorkshire Folk, Blues and Jazz Festival.

The name of the festival may seem a little staid to modern readers, but it's worth bearing in mind that even if the organisers had not genuinely had their roots in the folk music scene, it was a convention of the times that you never, ever, openly described your event as a rock festival. Even if all of your advertised acts were long-haired barbarians wielding electric axes and pounding drums at ferocious decibel levels, it was still the done thing to claim that it was a blues or jazz festival. This served the purpose of draping a thin veil of respectability over the orgy of free love, drug-taking, nudity, anarchy and profanity that was actually being promoted.

The site was secured in February 1970, and the pair wasted no time in announcing their plans. Indeed, Ripponden Urban Council was rather put out that they had not been contacted first, and convened a meeting to express their misgivings. "The thing which upsets residents in the district is that we are going to get a lot of people wandering about aimlessly, or otherwise," Councillor E Reed was reported as saying. "It's all very well to be 'with it'. But if you are actually 'with it' in Barkisland or Krumlin it might be most inconvenient."

"It's going to be bedlam up there," added Councillor J Dean. "They are going to need ambulances and who knows what. They have births at these things you know!"

The festival dates were announced for the weekend of August 15, and Highley and McEwen began approaching artists. Unfortunately, the major problem that would dog the event was apparent from the start: they had no funds, no capital and no financial backing. A launch gig at the Shay Club in Halifax, designed to raise funds and awareness, actually lost money. Although several backers were approached, none came through. A Mr Don Wilson had apparently agreed to invest £5000 in the festival, but pulled out at a point when it was too late for Highley and McEwen to do the same.

Originally the pair had imagined that this event might make them wealthy show-business impresarios. Now they just hoped they could make it through to the other side. They knew that this festival was the gamble of their lives, and decided early on that the only thing to do was to brazen it out with as much confidence, style and quick-witted dexterity as they could muster.

The first few tickets were sold, unadvertised, for a ridiculously low price of three shillings, in order to raise some initial funds. This money was needed to pay for advertising in order to put the first official tickets on sale, at a price of 30/-. It was announced that only a limited number would be available at this price and that after they had gone, the price would gradually go up to £3. This was a pioneering example of the kind of "early bird discount" tiered ticket pricing that is commonplace today.

Press releases were sent out claiming that this would be "the only festival in Britain to offer fifty hours of top bands, 150 acres of campsite, licensed bars, decent cheap food, free covered accommodation, beds for hire, all night concerts and boutiques."

An initial line-up was put together from McEwen and Highley's connections on the folk circuit, and the first 'name' band to be booked were Pentangle, the folk-jazz-pop supergroup featuring Bert Jansch, John Renbourn, Jacqui McShee, Danny Thompson and Terry Cox. In 1970 Pentangle were at the height of their success: their song, 'Light Flight' had been used as the theme for the BBC TV drama *Take Three Girls,* and their second album *Basket Of Light* had reached the top 5 at the end of 1969. Managed by the hard-nosed Jo Lustig, they were booked for £400, to be paid in advance.

Two popular singers and organ maestros, Alan Price and Georgie Fame, were also booked early on, costing £350 each. On March 14 the *Courier* reported that over 30 acts had been booked, naming Fairport Convention, Manfred Mann Chapter III, The Groundhogs, Ralph McTell, Champion Jack Dupree, The Mike Westbrook Big Band, The Alan Skidmore Quintet,

The Alex Welsh Band and Bonnie Dobson, in addition to the three acts detailed above.

"Although we are still negotiating, there appears to be little chance that The Beatles will appear," Derek McEwen is quoted as saying in the same article. It seems unlikely that anyone ever thought they would, given the Fab Four retired from live performance in 1966; in fact, Paul McCartney would announce that the band had broken up less than a month after this story appeared.

Although the quote is attributed to McEwen, this brilliant bit of misdirection sounds more characteristic of Brian Highley. While simply stating the true fact that the Beatles were highly unlikely to play, the name of the world's biggest group was nevertheless linked to the festival along with the tantalising suggestion that they *just might* turn up...

"The main artist, likely to be American, will be as big a draw as The Beatles, and will possibly appeal to a different musical public," McEwen (or Highley) concluded. He was most likely referring to The Grateful Dead, who Northern Entertainments had approached but, factoring in the cost of visas for the group and their sizable entourage, had been unable to afford.

Brian Highley struck a far better bargain when he secured an unknown artist called Elton John for the very reasonable sum of £75. Elton's debut album, *Empty Sky,* had been released the previous summer to general indifference, preceded by a handful of flop singles. Presumably because Elton's name would then have meant nothing to most music fans, it was conspicuously missing from an early flyer for the festival that announced a mostly folk-oriented bill.

PENTANGLE
The Johnstons
Ralph McTell
The Humblebums
Noel Murphy and Shaggis
FAIRPORT CONVENTION
Tony Capstick
Diz Disley

Johnny Silvo
Hamish Imlach
FOTHERINGAY
Christy Moore
Martyn Wyndham-Read
Dave Shannon and Sam Bracken
Roger Sutcliffe
Smiley
Marie Little
Gillian McPherson
Bonnie Dobson
The Jugular Vein Jug Band
Jo Ann Kelly
Foggy Dew-O
Dave Burland
Mike Harding
Champion Jack Dupree
Brett Marvin and the Thunderbolts
Alexis Korner and the New Church
Warm Dust
The Groundhogs
Jan Dukes De Grey
ALAN PRICE SET
GEORGIE FAME
Trader Horne
MANFRED MANN CHAPTER THREE
Mike Westbrook Band
Graham Bond
ALEX WELSH BAND

"Tickets are still on sale at ONLY 30/- for this, the most spectacular festival of popular music to be held in Britain in 1970, at KRUMLIN, BARKISLAND nr. Halifax- Yorkshire on 14th, 15th & 16th August, 1970. The BIG NAME who will top this fantastic bill has not yet been announced. But on the public announcement of the Top Billing, all 30/- tickets will be recalled and ticket prices will be increased to £3. Buy now and save money!"

PENTANGLE

JOHNSTONS
RALPH McTELL
HUMBLEBUMS
NOEL MURPHY AND
SHAGGIS

FAIRPORT CONVENTION

TONY CAPSTICK
DIZ DISLEY
JOHNNY SILVO
HAMISH IMLACH

FOTHERINGAY

CHRISTY MOORE
MARTYN
WYNDHAM-READ
DAVE SHANNON AND
SAM BRACKEN
ROGER SUTCLIFFE
SMILEY
MARIE LITTLE
GILLIAN McPHERSON
BONNIE DOBSON
JUGULAR VEIN JUG-BAND
JO-ANN KELLY
FOGGY DEW-O
DAVE BURLAND
MIKE HARDING
CHAMPION JACK DUPREE
BRETT MARVIN AND
THE THUNDERBOLTS
ALEXIS CORNER AND
THE NEW CHURCH
WARM DUST
GROUND HOGS
JAN DUKES DE GREY

Alan Price Set

Georgie Fame

TRADER HORNE

Manfred Mann

CHAPTER THREE
TREE
MIKE WESTBROOK BAND
GRAHAM BOND

Alex Welsh Band

yorkshire folk, blues & jazz festival

Tickets are **still** on

Sale at **only 30/-**

for this, the most spectacular Festival of Popular Music to be held in Britain in 1970, at

KRUMLIN, BARKISLAND

Nr. HALIFAX - YORKSHIRE

on

14th, 15th & 16th AUGUST, 1970

The **BIG-NAME** who will top this fantastic bill has not yet been announced.

but on the public announcement of the Top Billing, all 30/- tickets will be recalled and ticket prices will be increased to £3. Buy Now and Save Money !

For tickets or information apply:
P.O. BOX 5, SOWERBY BRIDGE, YORKSHIRE
(P.O., Cheque or M.O. made out to "Northern Entertainments", with S.A.E. please.)

Or your nearest Agent:

H.M.V. 363 OXFORD ST.,
LONDON, W1R 2BJ
01-629 1240

Won't Get Fooled Again

In March, the organisers held a public meeting at Barkisland School to reassure skittish local residents and hear their concerns. "These drop-outs and weirdies among the crowd will not be keen enough to withstand the rain, which might fall even though the affair takes place in August," one Mr A Symcock commented prophetically. He seemed to have confused an audience of middle-class college students with a pack of wild baboons, however. "They will break out of the ring fence which is being erected around the area and make for cover. This might mean breaking into property."

Fears of savage, rampaging weirdies notwithstanding, the locals and the council were eventually placated, the latter even expressing a vote of confidence praising the professionalism of Highley and McEwen. At this point the festival was being pitched as a two-day event, on Saturday and Sunday, but with a free night's entertainment for ticket holders on Friday. "It will be a festival in every sense of the word and I can see nothing but success for our ventures," Derek McEwen stated.

The *Courier* continued to print the pair's announcements and possible additions to the line-up. The Incredible String Band were mentioned early on, but were soon dropped from the bill and replaced by Trader Horne, Judy Dyble's post-Fairport Convention vehicle (in the end they too proved unavailable). A "pop ballet" was apparently commissioned from the Leeds-based acid-folk / prog-rock band Jan Dukes de Grey, to be performed by members of either the Royal Ballet or the Scottish National Ballet. At one point it was even suggested that the Woodstock Festival's lighting designer and onstage MC, Chip Monck, had come on board as an official adviser.

On May 9, the *Courier* broke the news that The Who had turned down a lucrative US tour to play at Krumlin. They were to headline the Saturday night concert, with another "even bigger" name promised for Sunday. The Who's set on Saturday would apparently include the world premiere of the band's next double-album, all two hours of it, which was due to be recorded prior to their appearance.

"Signing them has cost us well into four figures," Highley told the paper. "But they are worth it. Considering all the festival competition up and down the country this year they're a tremendous scoop for us. In fact, they've rejected events in Plumpton and the Isle of Wight, and a big American festival, to come to the West Riding. Obviously we're very thrilled about it – and very lucky!"

The same article also announced that Free had been added to the bill, but neither band would ultimately play. The saga of what exactly went down with The Who remains ambiguous. In his autobiography, *In Pursuit Of Trivia,* Brian Highley claims that he had received both verbal and written confirmation that The Who would play Krumlin, after their manager, Chris Stamp, visited the site and was satisfied that the event and the promoters were above board.

Highley suggests that Stamp was already in negotiations with the organisers of the much higher profile (and much bigger budget) 1970 Isle of Wight Festival for The Who to headline there, and that once that was confirmed they pulled out of Krumlin, as the contract with the IoW would have included an exclusivity clause, banning them from playing other festival shows that summer.

This sounds highly plausible, but during the bankruptcy hearings following the festival's collapse, Highley told a subtly different story. In this account, Highley and McEwen approached The Who and were contacted by a character named Cyrano claiming to be "in charge" of the group. He arrived with a man called David who said that he was The Who's road manager. This pair said that while contracts still needed to be signed by The Who's actual management, Northern Entertainments were free to announce that The Who would be appearing.

"It was later discovered that this man Cyrano had no right to offer The Who and quite a lot of adverse publicity followed," Highley said. "Some ticket refunds had to be made."

Most likely this was Dave 'Cyrano' Langston, the Who's first full-time road manager from 1965 to 1966, who remained close to the group long after he stopped working for them officially. Langston co-wrote the song 'Early Morning Cold Taxi' with Pete Townshend (recorded for *The Who Sell out* in 1967, but not included on the original track listing), and played guitar on John Entwistle's 1971 solo LP *Smash Your Head Against The Wall*.

The Who were advertised as headlining the festival until August 1, when *Melody Maker* ran a story on the event in which The Who stated that they'd never even been approached to play, let alone agreed, and made it clear that they had no intention of appearing. By this time the band was confirmed for the Isle of Wight Festival, which happened just two weeks after Krumlin. Incidentally, the double-album which Highley mentioned would most likely have been Pete Townshend's legendary but ill-fated *Lifehouse* project, which also never happened, although some of the songs turned up on The Who's next single album, *Who's Next,* in 1971.

Heavy Friends

In July, Ginger Baker's Air Force and Pink Floyd were added to a bill that also included The Pretty Things, Yes, Mungo Jerry, Atomic Rooster, Taste, Edgar Broughton, Quintessence, Juicy Lucy, Zoot Money and blues-rock band Steamhammer, as well as the acts already announced. Further down the bill were Amazing Blondel (briefly managed by Brian Highley), The Greatest Show On Earth, The National Head Band "with twenty heavy friends" and "Jan Dukes de Grey with seventy piece choir".

Most of the acoustic acts were now relegated to an "all-night folk and blues concert" in a separate marquee on Friday night, compered by singer-comedian and future *Last Of The Summer Wine* star Tony Capstick, who would introduce himself on stage as "Tony Cat's Prick". This line-up was still headlined by Noel Murphy and Shaggis who, for reasons best known to themselves, had been rechristened Draught Porridge, with the addition of former Strawbs bassist Ron Chesterman. Noel Murphy was an Irish singer and future comic actor; 'Shaggis' was banjo player Davey Johnstone, later to become Elton John's guitarist and, eventually, his long-term musical director, a position he still holds today.

"Word of mouth, a few handbills, one or two advertisements and a lot of lovely musicians have helped to sell the first 10,000 tickets," a leaflet proclaimed. One pictures the 'lovely musicians' (Elton John and Keith Moon, perhaps?) stumping door-to-door with guitars slung over their backs and books of tickets in hand, flogging them to the unwary. "By the time you read this, it is probable that the top act at this festival will have been announced."

By this point weekend tickets were £2 10s in advance and £3 on the day, although "it is just possible that some 30/- tickets may still be available, depending on how soon you read this notice."

That top act may have been Pink Floyd, although it's important to remember that back in 1970 the Floyd were not yet the massive draw they would soon become. They were still in the uneasy, experimental period between the departure of their frontman and main songwriter, the troubled psychedelic genius Syd Barrett, and the point where bassist Roger Waters seized control and, from 1973's *Dark Side Of The Moon* onwards, steered them to international stadium-straddling success.

In retrospect this period produced some of the band's most interesting and adventurous music, with albums like *Ummagumma, Atom Heart Mother* and *Meddle*. But in 1969-70 Pink Floyd were still playing a mix of Locarno and Top Rank ballrooms, provincial town halls and university student unions. Nevertheless, the prospect of the Pink Floyd of 1970 playing a lengthy, part-improvised set with full light show against the epic backdrop of the high Pennine hills was certainly an enticing one. Alas, it was not to be.

In his book, Brian Highley claims to have only had a verbal agreement with the band's management that was never officially confirmed. However, unlike The Who, Pink Floyd are profiled over several pages in the official festival programme, and the band are named as creditors in the bankruptcy proceedings that followed the event, suggesting that they were definitely booked to play, if not paid in advance.

Writing in the official festival programme, *Courier* journalist Gordon Pickles reflects the sense that in 1970 Pink Floyd were seen as a somewhat uncertain proposition. "They are full of experiment to the extent that they could make a complete lie out of anything I might write here," he confesses. "Dare I predict what they will come up with next?"

Pickles rolls up his sleeves and gives it his best shot. "They generate the same kind of excitement as Huxley on the science fiction. All the time they play you are plunged into a feeling of the afterworld, futuristic, to the real convert almost existentialist. The mood and atmosphere is thick and heavy you are left with a feeling that you pluck their music and cut into shreds of meaningful chunks of solid music. It's great and you just have to be involved."

A couple of paragraphs later, Pickles' fever seems to have passed as perhaps he starts to doubt whether the good people of Halifax are quite ready to start plucking and cutting meaningful chunks of solid music, or whatever it was, and attempts some cautious managing of expectations.

"Sure they must fail on occasion," he admits. "They are said to have failed at a recent festival at the Albert Hall. But let us put our hands together for a group prepared to try out new tactics, be aware of change and furthermore respond to it. I think every music lover should applaud their honesty of effort and their insatiable lust for work."

There you go: a bit weird and a bit hit or miss, but a hard-working band who try their best, something every decent northerner should approve of.

As well as The Grateful Dead, Northern Entertainments also pursued several other US acts, including Frank Zappa and The Turtles, but the cost of getting anyone over from the states was prohibitive. Nevertheless, according to Brian Highley's *In Pursuit Of Trivia*, negotiations to secure Captain Beefheart & The Magic Band for the princely sum of £2000 very nearly reached fruition.

Apparently all had proceeded satisfactorily over the phone, and Northern Entertainments secretary Katy Clay was asked to send written confirmation of the arrangements directly to the artist, known to his mum as Don Van Vliet. Unfortunately she addressed the envelope to a "Captain B. Fart" and began the enclosed covering letter "Dear Mr Fart…"

Although one would like to think that this would appeal to Captain Beefheart's surreal sense of humour it apparently did not, and no more was heard from him. Both Beefheart and The Grateful Dead would eventually play at the Bickershaw Festival, 35 miles to the west and 21 months later. This event was almost as disastrous as Krumlin and was promoted by future TV prankster Jeremy Beadle, who presumably at least managed to address the Captain by his preferred nomenclature.

A rumour persists too that Nick Drake played his last ever gig at the Krumlin Festival. There are no eyewitness accounts to confirm this, and even if he was an uncredited performer at the all-night folk concert it seems unlikely. Still, it's appropriate that this myth should attach itself to Krumlin, weaving the festival into the legend of the doomed, *poète maudit* singer-songwriter, whose own dark, romantic cult grows with each successive generation.

Various sources insist that Drake played at an open-air festival in Yorkshire in the spring of 1970, alongside Island Records labelmates Free. Of course Krumlin took place in mid-August, not spring, and although Free were mentioned as having been booked in the run-up to the festival they were never formally added to the bill, and certainly never played. But many of Drake's friends and collaborators did perform, such as Fairport Convention, Pentangle (with bassist Danny Thompson, who played on *Five Leaves Left*), and Fotheringay, who Drake had supported on a short British tour in March of that year.

Fans point to a photo showing a shadowy figure stage left, watching Pentangle on Saturday afternoon, claiming it bears a striking resemblance to Nick Drake. It's there if you want to see it, but in truth the figure could be anybody: a revenant or doppelganger, a ghost in the camera, a flickering interloper from the fringe.

Despite his posthumous fame, Nick Drake remains one of rock music's great enigmas. Never caught on moving film, his image can be seen in only a limited number of still photographs. Information about his life and career remains sketchy, too, especially where live performances are concerned.

Although he was signed to a major label and released three albums in his lifetime, there are less than 20 confirmed shows that Drake is known to have played. The last of these was supporting Ralph McTell (another Krumlin artist) at Ewell Technical College on June 25, 1970. If he had played at Krumlin in August, then it would certainly have been his last live show, as Drake retired into troubled seclusion from the winter of 1970, until his death from an overdose of antidepressants on November 25, 1974, at the age of 26. One imagines that playing at Krumlin could've convinced anyone that gigging and touring just weren't worth the effort, let alone as sensitive and haunted a soul as Nick Drake.

"And What A Hill It Was"

In the run-up to the event, all 30/- tickets were recalled by July 20, while a newsletter put out by Northern Entertainments advertised work for stewards on site at rates of either £2 or £3 per day. There was also a dubious request for "information and hospitality stewards (female) to work backstage, 24 hours per day, putting bands at ease and being generally helpful." A recent photograph was necessary when applying for this job, for which — despite the long hours — no pay was offered. Presumably it would be an honour and a privilege for any hippy rock chick worth the name to spend three or four days and nights hanging out with the bands backstage, rolling their joints, pouring their beers and generally keeping things mellow and groovy all round.

In a similar spirit, the souvenir programme featured a back cover photo of a comely young local lass posing in a tight-fitting *Yorkshire Folk, Blues and Jazz Festival* t-shirt and very little else. Unfortunately her mother took exception to a shadow in the photo that she mistook for a glimpse of pubic hair. Highley managed to take advantage of this controversy by promising to place large stickers over the offending photo, prompting a rush to secure sticker-free copies of the already-printed programme.

Meanwhile, the week before, the site was made ready. Locals remember roadies and "musicians who arrived early" (whoever heard of a musician arriving early for anything?) jamming on the stage as it was being set up. In fact the first sounds to come from the PA system were from records played on Thursday evening. The stage was assembled by a Wakefield scaffolding firm who were working from a rough sketch by Highley, as back then there were no commercially-available stages for outdoor amplified music festivals, or even an agreed-upon prototype for what they should be like.

The organisers also had to arrange for a road to be built so crews could gain access to the site, 60 trees to be felled and several dry stone walls to be demolished. The police, the Red Cross, the St John's Ambulance Brigade, the drugs charity

Release and of course the church all had their own service tents, and local Civil Aid units, from Yorkshire and nearby Rochdale, were brought in to help with communications, first aid and emergency food. A detailed report by Walter Lloyd, the chairman of Rochdale Civil Aid, is invaluable in describing the run-up to the festival, the unfolding disaster, and its aftermath.

Lloyd recalls that McEwen and Highley asked for the Civil Aid groups to help as they were catering for fifteen to twenty thousand people, but anticipated that attendance could reach as high as fifty thousand, which would put a great strain on their resources. Rochdale Civil Aid saw it as "a good opportunity to practice cooperation between regions," and Treasurer Ernie Flaherty met with Northern Entertainments, who asked if they could provide a soup kitchen capable of feeding 5000 people.

"We only had one Soyer boiler at the time, and to do 5000 portions in 24 hours or so really needed a second," the report notes. Luckily Ernie had the forethought to buy another in Lytham St Annes, and a cheque for £80 to buy bread and soup powder arrived from the organisers at the last minute. It would later bounce.

The Civil Aid Units were responsible for laying field communication cables around the site, so that officials could communicate by field telephone. Unfortunately, it was later found that Civil Aid members were the only ones who could get it together to operate them, and if they weren't permanently manning them, either there would be no-one to answer when a call was made, or the person at the other end would pick up the phone but not realise they had to press down the switch to make themselves heard.

A portable switchboard was set up at the Civil Aid headquarters in the stone barn adjoining the main farmhouse, which was at the very top of the steep hill farm that made up the festival site. "And what a hill it was," the report ominously notes. "The site was a typical Pennine hill farm, on steep hillside, with a narrow winding lane coming in at the top, no proper road down through the fields, only a path that would be suitable for pack ponies in dry weather."

"The land was infertile boulder clay, in an area of high rainfall, where every valley had its reservoir to feed the neighbouring industrial towns," the report continues. The colossal dam for the largest of these, the Scammonden Reservoir, was being constructed within earshot at the time; so too was the local stretch of the M62 motorway, connecting Yorkshire and Lancashire across the bleak Pennine moors.

The site did at least form a natural amphitheatre; on a good day, it must have seemed ideal. But it was also roughly a thousand feet above sea level, and west facing, that is exposed to the elements. As opposed to the comparatively sheltered Vale of York on the east side of the Pennines, the west side is at the mercy of the icy wind and rain blowing in from the North Sea and across the wilds of Lancashire.

The stage was set up at the bottom of the field, with backstage caravans behind it, and beyond that was the temporary ambulance station, set up in an old disused mill. The car park, with the police wireless caravan, was at the top of the hill, behind the farmhouse; camping was in adjoining fields, and the whole area was fenced off with scaffolding and chain link netting. "Around the edges were marquees for selling food and beer and jewellery, candles, 'underground' magazines and camping equipment," the Civil Aid report dispassionately notes.

Perhaps unwisely, the main toilet block was also placed at the very top of the hill, while the site plan in the official programme clearly shows three large sleeping marquees at the top of the campsite, just below Firth House. These are not mentioned in the account of the disaster that followed, so it's uncertain as to whether they were ever actually erected. Strangely the large inflatable marquee in which the folk concert took place isn't shown on the site map, but this was definitely there, and would play an important role over the weekend.

44

yorkshire folk, blues & jazz festival 1970

Souvenir Brochure 3/=

PROGRESSIVE POP & BLUES

THE WHO
MANFRED MANN
CHAPTER 3
MUNGO JERRY
GEORGIE FAME
ALAN PRICE
GREATEST SHOW
ON EARTH
JO-ANN KELLY
CHAMPION JACK DUPREE
BRETT MARVIN &
THE THUNDERBOLTS
THE HUMBLEBUMS
ALEXIS KORNER
GROUND HOGS
WARM DUST
JAN DUKES DE GREY

FOLK & JAZZ

PENTANGLE
FAIRPORT CONVENTION
FOTHERINGAY
THE JOHNSTONS
RALPH McTELL
GRAHAM BOND
ALEX WELSH
MIKE WESTBROOK
CONCERT ORCHESTRA
DRAUGHT PORRIDGE
AMAZING BLONDEL
FOGGY DEW-O
JUGULAR VEIN JUG BAND
DAVE SHANNON &
SAM BRACKEN
CHRISTY MOORE
GILLIAN McPHERSON
and many others

IMAGINATION HAS BEEN CAUGHT

ENTHUSIASM FIRED

FESTIVAL FEVER RUNS HIGH

LOCAL, NATIONAL AND MUSICAL PRESS ALIKE HAVE ACCLAIMED THIS AS THE BEST BALANCED FESTIVAL OF THE YEAR

yorkshire folk, blues & jazz festival

Krumlin, Barkisland

14, 15 & 16 AUGUST 1970

Word of mouth, a few handbills, one or two advertisements and a lot of lovely musicians have helped to sell the first 10,000 tickets (at only **30/–** for the whole weekend !).

By the time you read this, it is probable that the top act at this Festival will have been announced, whereupon ticket prices will be as follows:

Weekend tickets in advance	£2 10s 0d
Weekend tickets on the day	£3 0s 0d
Sunday only, tickets in advance	£1 10s 0d
Sunday only, tickets on the day	£2 0s 0d

However, it is just possible that some 30/– tickets may still be available – depending on how soon you read this notice.

In either case, rush your crossed P.O./M.O./Cheque (made payable to 'Northern Entertainments') to :

NORTHERN ENTERTAINMENTS

P.O. BOX 5   SOWERBY BRIDGE   YORKSHIRE

Or your nearest Agent :

JOHN E. CROWTHER PRINTING SERVICE, RIPPONDEN, Nr. HALIFAX   TEL. 2172

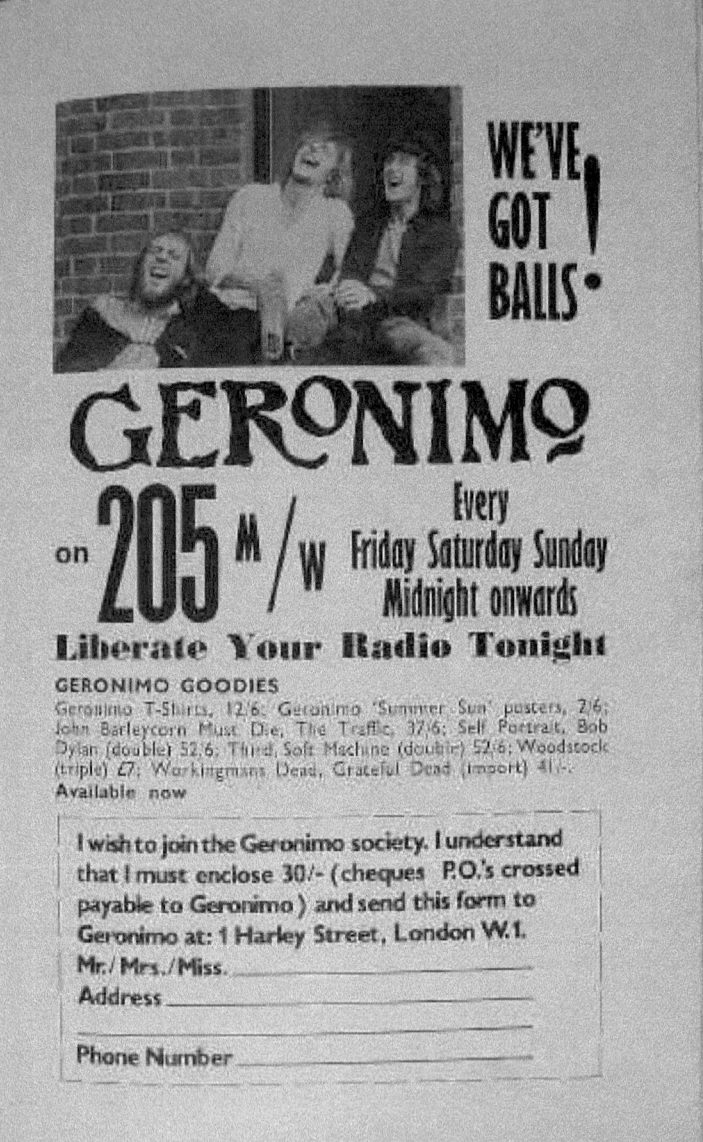
48

Misty Water

In July, bar licenses were granted, permitting the sale of canned beer and draught ale in plastic cups from 4-11pm on Friday, 11-3 and 5-11 on Saturday, and 11-3 and 5-10.30 on Sunday. The beer tents out front were run by Jack Bunting, landlord of the Upper George pub in Halifax (the favoured watering hole of the town's folkie, hippy and biker communities) while the backstage bar, which had an extension till 1am each night, was run by Brian Wickham of the Fleece Inn in Barkisland.

Around the same time the local council insisted that the organisers needed to provide 100,000 gallons of water per day that was suitable for public consumption, an estimate based on an expected turnout of 50,000 people needing two gallons each for drinking and washing. Highley and McEwen thought this somewhat excessive, and both the expected attendance and requirements per day seem to have been revised downwards soon after. But a large amount of drinking water was still urgently needed, in the days when it could not just simply be bought in bottles.

To further complicate matters, Banquet House Farm was not then on the mains water supply and all its needs were provided by a moorland stream running through the property. There was however a supply from the Wakefield Water Board nearby, which could provide up to 10,000 gallons per day. When Northern Entertainments proposed making up the rest by using the stream to fill reserve tanks, and to pipe the water from there to taps around the site, the council medical officer was sceptical.

To counter this, a *Courier* news story appeared, showing farm owner Neil Hirst with his wife and three young children. Hirst was quoted as saying he'd lived on the farm for 25 years and that the spring had been its only water supply "since before living memory." All his children had drunk it since birth and they were as fit as fiddles, he insisted. The article asserted that "private bacteriological tests" were being carried out. These apparently proved favourable: "The spring water is far better than that which runs out of any tap in Halifax," the analyst told the paper in a follow-up report.

Decades later, Brian Highley admitted that this "expert analyst" was in fact a completely unqualified friend of his, wearing a white hospital coat for the benefit of reporters. The stream was duly diverted into pipes and huge water tanks set up, but at the beginning of August Ripponden medical officer Dr S H Brook found that the spring actually was infected and couldn't be used after all. At the eleventh hour, an agreement was made with Calderdale Water Board to transport the necessary supplies from nearby reservoirs by tanker, to complement the amount already being provided by Wakefield Water Board.

Although they may have been suspicious at first, it seems that as the date approached the local authorities were swept up in the excitement and did all they could to help the festival succeed. No doubt they anticipated the money, trade and prestige such an event could bring into the local area, and the more celebrity names were linked to Krumlin, the more this glamour pertained.

On August 8 the *Courier* gleefully gossiped that Lulu and her husband, Bee Gee Maurice Gibb, had bought tickets for the festival, while — in an echo of the earlier Beatles non-story — Brian Highley was found denying supposed rumours that the Rolling Stones would be appearing. "We might get the Stones for the festival," he said, a week before the event was due to take place. "We are definitely trying and, at this moment, actually negotiating with them. However it is not true to say they are booked."

When it became clear that The Who would not be playing, Northern Entertainments attempted to secure The Kinks as a last-minute replacement. They were added to the bill as Saturday headliners, but it seems contracts were never finalised, as the day before the festival was due to start it was announced in the national music press that they wouldn't be appearing after all. This was an unfortunate blow for the organisers that they rightly anticipated would impact on walk-up sales. However, far worse was to come.

We Hope You Will Enjoy The Show

The official program or "Souvenir Brochure" for the Yorkshire Folk, Blues and Jazz Festival, edited by Gordon Pickles and sold for 3/-, listed the finalised running order (from top of the bill down) as follows.

Friday 3pm - midnight

The Pretty Things
Zoot Money
Atomic Rooster
Elton John
Groundhogs
Juicy Lucy
Georgie Fame

Following this there will be an all-night folk concert in a giant marquee:

Draught Porridge
Tony Capstick
Diz Disley
Johnny Silvo & Dave Moses
Hamish Imlach
Christy Moore
Martyn Wyndham-Read
Roger Sutcliffe
Smiley
Marie Little
Foggy Dew-O
Dave Burland
Mike Harding
The Honeydew

Saturday 10am - midnight

The Who
Manfred Mann Chapter III
Fotheringay
Alan Price
Graham Bond Organisation
Fairport Convention
Pentangle
Amazing Blondel
Ralph McTell
Jo Ann Kelly
Brett Marvin and the Thunderbolts
The Humblebums
Alexis Korner and the New Church
Dave Shannon and Sam Bracken
Gillian McPherson
The Johnstons
Jugular Vein Jug Band
Pink Floyd

Sunday 10am - midnight

Ginger Baker's Airforce
Quintessence
Edgar Broughton Band
Mungo Jerry
Taste
National Head Band
Greatest Show On Earth
Warm Dust
Jan Dukes De Grey
Yes
Steam Hammer
Mike Westbrook
Alex Welsh Band

"Compering the shows will be Gerry Floyd most of the time with Pete Drummond coming in on Sunday to help out."

"Gerry" (actually Jerry) Floyd was the resident DJ at London's Marquee club and one of the top 'underground' disc jockeys of the time. He would later be an early convert to punk, playing the Vortex and the Roxy Club alongside Don Letts, before sadly dying of a brain haemorrhage in the early eighties. At Krumlin, fans remember Floyd repeatedly playing 'The Ballad of Marmalade Emma and Teddy Grimes' by Hard Meat, and being dragged from his decks on Friday night when he had the temerity to point out the plain-clothed police to the audience.

Warning them to be on their guard, Floyd referred to one disguised officer in particular as a "ginger-haired pig" and was fined £25 by a magistrate at the same Saturday morning emergency court mentioned earlier. He was however able to resume his onstage duties later that day.

Pete Drummond was a Radio DJ and broadcaster who had moved from the pirate Radio London to become part of the original Radio 1 team in 1967, where he was the main presenter of the progressive *Top Gear* radio show, alongside John Peel. Peel eventually took over *Top Gear* while Drummond moved on to the equally adventurous *Sounds Of The Seventies* show, until it was axed in 1975. As things turned out, it's unlikely he actually made it up to Krumlin.

Looking at the rest of the line-up, what's most surprising is the suggestion that Pink Floyd were to go on first on Saturday, at 10am, but surely this was never the intention. Listed after them are The Johnstons, a popular close harmony Irish folk band led by siblings Adrienne and Michael, and also featuring guitarist Paul Brady. When The Johnstons split in 1974, Brady would join Christy Moore in folk supergroup Planxty before going on to a very successful solo career. In 1981 Adrienne Johnston died in a mysterious accident, with some believing she was murdered.

Gillian McPherson, later known as Gillie McPherson, is an Irish singer-songwriter perhaps best known for her folky 1971 album for RCA, *Poets And Painters And Performers Of Blues*. She briefly had her own BBC2 TV show in the seventies and is still going strong, mixing up blues, jazz and rock in her writing and performances. Dave Shannon and Sam Bracken were also Irish folk singers who mixed blues and jazz into their repertoire; soon after playing Krumlin, they joined with singer Fiona Simpson to form the trio Therapy.

Brett Marvin & The Thunderbolts were a long-running country-pub-blues band featuring future hit-maker Jona Lewie ('Stop The Cavalry', 'You'll Always Find Me In The Kitchen At Parties'). A six-piece, none of whom were called Brett Marvin, they had a #2 novelty hit in 1972 under the name of Terry Dactyl & The Dinosaurs, with the Lewie-penned 'Seaside Shuffle' — a jug band number in a similar vein to Mungo Jerry's 'In The Summertime'.

Although she never achieved major success, Jo Ann Kelly is considered to have been one of the very best English female blues singers. In the late sixties she worked with both Tony 'TS' McPhee of the Groundhogs and Brett Marvin & The Thunderbolts; tragically she died of a brain tumour in 1990, aged just 46. Amazing Blondel were a hippy-folk trio from Scunthorpe that played their own songs in a renaissance style on authentic period instruments, creating a fey, acoustic sound not dissimilar to The Incredible String Band or early Tyrannosaurus Rex. Signing to Island Records, they released several albums throughout the seventies, much acclaimed by fans of acid-folk and English progressive music.

Manfred Mann Chapter Three were led by the titular keyboard player and drummer Mike Hugg, both formerly of the similarly-named sixties pop band, but traded in experimental jazz-rock that bore little relation to the 'Doo Wah Diddy Diddy' hitmakers. Releasing two fine albums, they were a short-lived interlude before the formation of the more conventional Manfred Mann's Earth Band in 1971, later to hit the top 10 with 'Blinded By The Light' and 'Davy's On The Road Again'.

Trad jazz singer and trumpeter Alex Welsh was down to open Sunday's line-up, followed by the more progressive jazz of the great Mike Westbrook. Promoting their second album *Time And A Word,* Yes would have been quite the draw at Krumlin, with new guitarist Steve Howe (ex-Tomorrow) having only recently joined Jon Anderson, Chris Squire, Bill Bruford and Tony Kaye.

Warm Dust are among the handful of bands profiled in the programme, where they are described as playing "free music". "They say they gain ideas for their music from the scream of the group van gearbox, the noise of an unoiled door or the dripping of a tap... some people find it almost too underground to listen to." In fact, Warm Dust were a tight, high-energy jazz-rock band, notable for featuring future Ace, Squeeze, Mike & The Mechanics and successful solo singer Paul Carrack on keyboards and backing vocals.

Greatest Show On Earth were a prog-rock band with a horn-led sound similar to Blood, Sweat & Tears, and released two albums for Harvest in 1970. They featured a teenage Norman Watt-Roy and his older brother Garth, and had a European hit with the single 'Real Cool World'. Norman Watt-Roy later formed Loving Awareness, who evolved into The Blockheads after teaming up with ex-Kilburn & The High Roads singer Ian Dury. He went on to become a leading session bassist in the post-punk era.

National Head Band were a hard rock outfit who recorded one album for Warner's in 1971. Taste were of course the great Irish blues-rock band led by up-and-coming guitar hero Rory Gallagher, who would depart for a solo career by the end of the year. The Edgar Broughton Band and Quintessence both hailed from the Notting Hill Gate freak scene, and were festival staples of the era.

Northern Entertainments had got very lucky with Mungo Jerry. Signing them up as relative unknowns, they watched as the band's debut single 'In The Summertime' shot to number one and stayed there for seven weeks in the run-up to Krumlin. It would become one of the biggest-selling singles ever, and for a brief period Mungo-mania gripped the nation. Although they had several more hit singles through the early seventies, Mungo Jerry are now mostly remembered for that one song, ultimately a novelty hit; but at the time many believed that they could be the new Beatles.

Former Cream and Blind Faith drummer Ginger Baker had formed sprawling jazz-rock supergroup Air Force at the end of 1969. They featured Steve Winwood (organ) and Ric Grech (bass/violin) from Blind Faith; Traffic's Chris Wood, plus Graham Bond and Harold McNair as saxophonists; former Moody Blues and future Wings guitarist Denny Laine; American singer Jeanette Jacobs; and no less than three drummers (Baker, Phil Seaman and Alan White) plus percussionist Remi Kabaka. Of course, ultimately none of the bands booked for Sunday got to play.

Alongside the running order in the programme is an intriguing note. "Incidentally there are three top rated groups standing to one side to take the place of anyone who for any reason has to pull out." But elsewhere a degree of patience and understanding is called for.

"There has never been a festival at which all bands advertised to appear have actually performed their full act at the time programmed," the programme cautions. "We are bound to have hang-ups. We have over 50 hours of contracted entertainment and only 40 hours of official playing time. All of the bands should play, all of the bands should play on time but this is going to mean programming some of them to play throughout the night. If bands are late arriving it could be the traffic (although we hope to overcome this problem, if we can get a heliport license for the backstage area). Please keep cool."

The programme introduction also tries hard to make the fact that a motorway is being built nearby and within earshot into a selling point. "In the distance you will have a unique opportunity of seeing man's eternal effort to control this wild environment. Work is in progress at this moment on the new Yorkshire to Lancashire motorway— the M62.

"The scene is a full one. With the modern echo of roaring bulldozers faintly heard in the background and the view of a heavily eroded hill setting all around, we are presented with a complete picture of the age we live in."

As well as profile features on Fairport Convention, Fotheringay, The Honeydew, Mungo Jerry, 'The' Pentangle, Pink Floyd, Quintessence, Ralph McTell and Warm Dust, there is an ad for Radio Geronimo and a hand-drawn map of the site. The information pages are appropriately informative, starting with a few words on the site.

"At first glance the Krumlin site may not look good but as you get to know the area you will find that the unique combination of flat land and steeply sloping hills offers perfect views of the stage and plenty of decent camping ground. We have included a map of the site in this programme but from experience we know that these maps rarely bear any resemblance to the reality, we would, therefore, suggest that you stroll around and find things. Somewhere you will find the following:

"300 toilets (to be emptied continuously throughout the festival period), litter bins (please use them), sleep marquees, bus seats for hire, these make good beds and will cost only 8/- for the three days, bars, food, first aid posts, record shops, leather shops, posters, clothes, washing facilities, strolling players, instant audience participation theatre, drinking water."

The fuzz: "Honest, they've been very helpful throughout… please cooperate with them."

The bars: "will be open for longer than normal licensed hours but there will be dry periods during the day and throughout the night. The bar license will stretch only as far as the entrance of the marquee in which drinks are being sold. No-one can stop you buying cans by the dozen and taking them out of the bar.

"Please don't do your nut if the bars run out of beer. Deliveries will be made throughout the weekend. If you can, buy your weekend's beer in one lot to save the blockages which will occur if everyone is going to the bar for individual half pint cans."

The page concludes with pleas to refrain from climbing the pylon or interfering with the farm animals, and to please note that car parking has to be paid for and is run as a separate concern to the festival, by local farmers. Has everybody got that? Okay, let's get on with the show…

Krumlin on Saturday afternoon. Photo by Annie Fair

The Gates Of Eden

Thursday night saw a reception on site for press and local dignitaries, with a buffet and free bar, but campers had started to arrive at Krumlin from early in the week. It was a typically youthful crowd, taking advantage of the long school and university summer break to travel not only from across Yorkshire and the north, but from further afield as well. Many hitch-hiked up from London or down from Scotland, while others arrived in 'borrowed' cars (parents/owners not informed). Some travelled from Europe, America and even Africa to be there, with plans to go on to the Isle of Wight Festival ten days later.

A worrying number turned up dressed only in jeans and t-shirts; the lucky ones had ex-army greatcoats. Most brought sleeping bags, but many didn't bother with tents. It was midsummer after all, and hadn't the advertisements promised free covered accommodation and beds for hire, if need be? They arrived in Halifax where a special festival bus service was laid on to take them to the site. Typically, this was more expensive than the regular bus, which would have been going that way anyway.

On Friday morning the sky was overcast but the day stayed mostly dry, although Duncan Smyth, reviewing the festival for the *Courier,* remembered one downpour in the afternoon before the bands started, and the odd shower thereafter. But although it was not yet raining consistently the wind was picking up, causing temperatures to plummet, especially once the sun went down.

The organisers were relying on significant numbers paying on the gate in order to supply the ready cash needed to pay the artists. While some had received money in advance, many more expected to be given their agreed fee in cash either just before or just after they went on stage. Unfortunately, local lads employed as gate stewards and stage crew were letting all their mates in for free, and a huge number of forged tickets were circulating, printed locally and sold through no less than 14 different pirate ticket agencies and small ads in the pages of *Melody Maker,* as well as on site. These were eventually identified, and were not accepted at the turnstiles, while the gang responsible for selling them in the car park was rounded up. But the damage to gate profits was already done.

While Brian Highley ran the backstage area and dealt with the press and media, Derek McEwen handled the finances and so was the first to realise just how deep in the shit they really were. It was later recounted that McEwen had taken on 60 gate stewards "without checking their integrity" as they had been recommended by ticket agents. Some even remember a heavy mob of modern jazz-loving bouncers shaking down the weekend hippies at the gates for an extra charge, while mocking the dreary folk acts they'd come to see. Only a swiftly-delivered monologue on the merits of Ornette Coleman could get you past these toughs unscathed — echoes of Peter Shertser's notorious East London 'mutant mod' crew The Firm, with their endless hustling, barracking and piss-taking of UFO club regulars, as recounted in Jonathan Green's *A Day in the Life.*

Others remain convinced that security was being handled by the Hell's Angels but, although this was the case at other festivals in both the US and UK around this time, it definitely wasn't being done at Krumlin.

"No Hell's Angels were involved at any stage," Brian Highley insists. "This is an urban myth that probably developed because Dave Jack, a friend who was involved in backstage security, wore a leather jacket and had the hairy-faced look then associated with Hell's Angels."

They may not have been invited officially, but several festival-goers remember the presence of a distinct biker contingent among the audience. This was supposedly led by a mountainous figure with one wooden leg and a German army helmet, who cruised through the churned-up mud on a large bike with a sidecar. When a biker-approved band such as The Pretty Things or The Groundhogs took the stage, he would dismount to dance by planting his wooden leg into the ground like a tent pole and charging wildly round it in circles.

Eighteen-year-old Clive Heenan recalls on one occasion the wooden leg was actually planted on his foot. "I didn't like to say anything; after what seemed like hours he leaned over and I managed to retrieve it. When it rained, they just threw a tarpaulin over him. He just sat there for two days. One can only imagine his toilet breaks."

The Groundhogs' TS McPhee heard rumours that a "Yorkshire Mafia" was demanding protection money from the various stallholders around the site. This was actually a mob that came up from London specifically to shake down legitimate traders. They were checked on the Friday night and the ringleaders were arraigned at an emergency magistrates' session in Halifax on Saturday morning, before being properly tried and convicted in Leeds several months after the festival ended.

Apart from the weather, one of the most-repeated complaints about the festival concerned the prices being charged by stallholders for food and other everyday essentials. While today's festival-goers have become inured to the huge mark-ups common at such events, back then there was still an expectation that such things should be affordable, particularly at an event that to some extent traded on the credentials of the underground— and particularly, perhaps, in Yorkshire.

In fact, as Brian Highley recalls, cheap food was available, courtesy of "local jazz musician, publican and concert promoter" Roddy Marshall, who set up a marquee stocked with several thousand tins of baked beans and a couple of vats of boiling water. For a nominal fee he would place a tin into an old washing boiler, heat it in the water and then hand it over wrapped in a paper towel to prevent burns. Can openers were attached to the counter with string to prevent theft, but a plastic spoon was included in the price. It seems his venture wasn't a great success as he still had cupboards full of beans for years to come after the festival. His marquee proved most popular when he allowed rain-soaked campers to shelter in it on Saturday night.

There were 50 uniformed police officers on site and another 50 in reserve, all of which the organisers were expected to pay for, as well as an undisclosed number of plain-clothed officers from the drug squad. The latter were identifiable by the fact of their "all wearing the same army and navy combat jackets and being five stone heavier than anyone else" (Dennis Poole). Their numbers may have been significant, but there are no reports of them being heavy-handed. Despite dope and acid being, by other accounts, widely available and enjoyed by many present, there were only ten reported drug busts.

"The fuzz" later gave a conservative estimate of attendance figures at 15-20,000; press reports would claim 25,000 or more. Certainly, the number of people on site compared to the number of advance tickets sold suggested that the money paid on the gate would more than cover the organisers' pressing expenses. So when Derek McEwen set off to the several ticket booths on Friday afternoon to collect the first lot of takings, he optimistically expected to pick up around £5000 in total. Returning with just £48, he saw the abyss yawning open before him. It was at this point that Derek McEwen started to feel decidedly unwell.

Bad Side Of The Moon

The music was supposed to start at three, but by then the main stage and toilet facilities were still being constructed. None of the food concessions had yet opened, leaving many fans who had been there all day with nothing to do but drink and smoke on an empty stomach (they may have neglected to bring their own food, but had all stocked up on weed and cheap cider). Most of the advertised bands hadn't yet turned up either, and those who had were arguing amongst themselves as to the running order, which had not yet been fixed. A state-of-the-art electronic message board above the stage showed continual, and increasingly fantastical, updates on the line-up. 'Headline band still to be announced!' the message board flashed, while the restless crowd waited to see if any kind of band at all would materialise.

Finally, at some point between five and eight o'clock in the evening - accounts differ - The Humblebums started playing. Billy Connolly and Gerry Rafferty's folk duo weren't actually meant to perform until Saturday, but arrived early and amidst all the confusion and disagreement they drew the short straw and were immediately shoved onstage.

Although it stayed dry, temperatures were already dropping dramatically by the time of Elton John's early evening set. Nevertheless, most attendees remember him as the highlight of the weekend. Krumlin was Elton's first ever outdoor festival show, and he was still a relative unknown, playing a set made up of Rolling Stones covers ('Honky Tonk Women') and material from *Elton John* and his yet-to-be-released breakthrough album, *Tumbleweed Connection*. 'Border Song,' 'Sixty Years On' and 'Bad Side Of The Moon' were singled out by an anonymous reviewer for the weekly music press, which also quoted an awestruck audience member comparing Elton to "a white, male Aretha Franklin."

Accompanied by bassist Dee Murray and drummer Nigel Olsson, Elton must have seen Krumlin as an important, make or break opportunity to prove himself to the festival freaks and the counterculture crowd. By all accounts he played a blinder, winning over the whole field against the odds and even passing out plastic beakers of warming brandy to the front rows.

"I hope this dispels the myth that I'm Radio One Club and Tony Blackburn," Elton boasted at the climax of his set. To his satisfaction, he was called back for an encore. Almost immediately afterwards he would set out on his first US tour, including his legendary August 25 debut at the Troubadour Club in West Hollywood, the beginning of a short residency there that would make him a major star almost literally overnight – one of twenty concerts that changed the world, according to *Rolling Stone* in 1990.

Melody Maker's Chris Charlesworth, who had grown up in nearby Skipton and cut his teeth as pop writer on Bradford's *Telegraph & Argus*, was covering the festival alongside his colleague Andrew Means. He was particularly struck by Elton's set.

"On he came, dressed up very flash, and he pounded hell out of that piano for an hour or so," Chris wrote. "I had never heard his music before, but I thought he was absolutely fantastic. All those miserable people in that field… by the time they had finished their set, they were happy. He got some bottles of brandy and loads of plastic cups, and he handed out brandy to the people in the crowd, saying 'Sorry about the weather, it's not my fault, but I'll do the best I can to keep you warm so, there you go, some brandy.' That went down extremely well."

(Quoted from *Elton- the biography* by David Buckley, Carlton Books 2007).

Chris Charlesworth introduced himself to Elton backstage, where he supposedly found him sharing a drink with Sandy Denny in a caravan, although Brian Highley is sure that Denny didn't turn up until Saturday. Conducting a mini-interview on the spot, Chris enthused about Elton's performance, both in person and in the following week's *Melody Maker*, which established a very useful friendship between the young rock writer (soon to become *MM's* man in New York through the early seventies), and the budding superstar of the new decade, who would always remember the kid who gave him his first rave review.

Georgie Fame drew the short straw in having to follow Elton: the title of his then-current single, 'Somebody Stole My Thunder' could not have been more apt. Ever the consummate professional, Fame doubtless did his best, and was probably glad not to have to deal with any actual thunderstorms — yet.

As darkness fell, the heavy rockers took over. Atomic Rooster were led by the troubled Vincent Crane on manic overdriven organ and occult, death-obsessed vocals. Their ominous, over-wrought anthems never sounded more atmospheric than on a cold, dark Pennine hillside, and like Elton they too were rewarded with an encore. The band would release their second album, *Death Walks Behind You,* the following month, and went on to have a couple of hit singles in 1971, 'Tomorrow Night' and 'Devil's Answer'. They broke up in 1975 and, after a troubled few years which included a brief period playing keyboards in Dexy's Midnight Runners, Crane took his own life in 1989.

In August 1970 The Pretty Things were at their psychedelic peak, yet ironically they were also on the verge of disintegration due to the commercial failure of their latterly acclaimed masterpieces, 1968's haunting yet electrifying rock opera *SF Sorrow* and its recently-released follow-up, *Parachute.* Rather the worse for wear due to strong drink and possibly other substances, they gave a powerful if ragged performance, in what should have been Friday night's headlining set.

In fact that honour went to blues rockers Juicy Lucy, newly formed from the ashes of terminally unlucky Californian expats and John Peel favourites The Misunderstood, and still featuring slide guitar genius Glenn Ross Campbell. They had been meant to go on in the afternoon, but insisted on a later slot as they were still riding high on the back of their sole hit single, a lengthy workout on Bo Diddley's 'Who Do You Love?' which had reached number 14 in the UK charts in February 1970. The change-over worked well, and Juicy Lucy provided a fitting climax to Friday night.

The Groundhogs on stage

The Loneliest Man In The World

The all-night folk and blues concert in the inflatable marquee was a popular draw, as it offered some shelter from the cold winds blowing up outside. Highlights included Hamish Imlach, fresh from an attempt to climb the central pole of the backstage beer tent, fuelled by a bottle of brandy provided by Elton John, and Johnny Silvo coming on in a kilt and announcing himself as the only genuine member of the Black Watch Regiment (the Highland soldiers famed for their fierceness in battle, and for never wearing any underwear beneath their regimental kilts).

On Saturday morning Brian Highley had to attend an emergency court session in Halifax to deal with ticket forgers, the protection mob threatening traders, and errant DJ Jerry Floyd, who Highley bailed out and brought back to the site at around 11am. It was then that Derek McEwen's disappearance became apparent. No-one had seen him since the previous evening, and it had been assumed that he'd driven into town with Highley.

Others thought that McEwen had left with the boss of the scaffolding company, who had also disappeared from the site, leaving his employees disorganised and unpaid. Rumours began to circulate that McEwen had made off with the money, when in fact the takings at the gate had already disappeared by the time he went to collect them. The problem was made worse by ticketless fans taking advantage of holes in the fence, as the scaffolding crew refused to repair them until they were paid (and the man responsible for paying them had buggered off).

Most were sympathetic however, and were worried that McEwen had suffered a nervous breakdown. It was feared that he might be wandering the moors alone, on a cold night and what looked to be an unsettled day at best. But serious concerns over McEwen's welfare necessarily had to be put to one side as Brian Highley, already working to the point of exhaustion after very little sleep, was now running the festival virtually single-handed.

According to Walter Lloyd, of Rochdale Civil Aid, "as so often happens during a time of crisis, fresh leaders emerged, and these formed themselves into a new management." He lists these as Huw Price, the stage manager; John Gawkroger who had come in at the last moment to oversee the ticket sellers; Brian Wickham, who had the backstage beer tent concession; and Les (or Lee) Allen, a London booking agent who was able to negotiate with the groups he represented.

Brian Highley paints a slightly different picture to the one outlined by the Civil Aid report, pointing out that he was left in more-or-less sole charge of the backstage area while Civil Aid were mainly concerned with the campsite, and as such were less aware of what was going on elsewhere. Highley recounts how his wife, Kaye, the company secretary Katy Clay and Brian Wickham formed a committee operating from the farmhouse at the top of the hill to deal with the situation in the main arena.

Brian Wickham, who was also the landlord of the Fleece Inn at Barkisland, advanced money from his bar takings to pay the expenses, if not the fees, of the bands present. According to their report, Civil Aid members went out selling programmes to ensure the stewards were paid enough to be able to eat (despite being promised free meals, in the event they were expected to feed themselves). Volunteers from the Release tent (there to offer drug and legal advice) apparently did the same.

The gang responsible for forged ticket sales had been "located and checked," and although Walter admits that they had already had a disastrous effect on ticket receipts, at this stage he was optimistic. "By dark, confidence had been restored among the groups and the staff, and the future of the festival was assured — it was expected to at least break even as a result of Sunday ticket sales, with the faint possibility of a large profit."

Alas, this was not to be. Already the Civil Aid report reads like a military document, with its talk of restoring morale, establishing a chain of command, checking enemy forces and shoring up defences. Soon it would come to seem more like The Charge of The Light Brigade.

Flowers In The Rain

Mike Taylor: "At some point during the music we erected a fly sheet over our ground sheet to save us from the rain, and as we were on a slope the rain washed off the end of the fly sheet and onto the foot part of our sleeping bags. The night hours were measured by regular reports from my cohabiting friends about the progress of the wetness from foot to midriff. Come first light we were all cold, wet and confused."

Starting early in the afternoon, rather than the over-optimistic 10am suggested in the programme, Saturday's main stage line-up continued the folky theme with sets from the unsung "queen of British country blues," Jo Ann Kelly, and Ralph McTell. McTell had actually been paid his fee that morning, on the insistence of his agent Jo Lustig, who was present, but quietly returned it to Brian Highley later on, telling him to "put it in the pot." He was followed by Irish close harmony folk group The Johnstons, and Rochdale-based folk-pop trio The Honeydew, who released a single, 'All Part Of The Game', and an eponymous LP on the Argo label that same year.

According to contemporary reviews, intermittent showers were already starting to fall, and it was not warm. Some enterprising soul provided giant orange plastic bags, the size of a half pig apparently, which those audience members lucky enough to get climbed into (in some cases putting them over the top of their sleeping bags), and simply laid down in them to watch the bands. These primitive accessories probably saved hundreds from exposure, and the 'Krumlin bag' was a badge of survival and fortitude carried proudly by many to festivals in the following years.

Pentangle, whose management had made sure they were paid well in advance, earned a warm reception for a strong set drawn largely from their *Basket Of Light* album. But because of the general disorganisation, arguments over the running order and the news that no-one was going to be paid, most of the bands had retreated to the backstage hospitality tent for several hours. Fairport Convention were apparently the worst casualties, eventually swerving onto the stage at five in the afternoon with instruments in one hand and pints in the other.

Guitarist Simon Nicol approached the microphone. "Ello, ello, we've been in the beer tent since two, and they said you're on in half an hour, so we thought we'd better get them in, and then they said you're on in half an hour, so we thought we'd better get them in, and then they said you're on in half an hour..."

He was pulled away from the microphone and the band launched into what was, against all odds, an electrifying set, though not without further mishaps. Richard Thompson remembers that while the rest of the band were playing the sensitive Irish ballad, 'A Bonnie Bunch of Roses,' Simon was sat cross-legged in front of his amplifier, playing an Indian raga in a different key. "So we had to sort of kick him and unplug him."

Bassist Dave Pegg, meanwhile, was so much the worse for wear due to drink that he actually shat himself on stage and continued playing. Even more unfortunately, he was wearing a pair of white trousers, the rear of which were soon stained a nasty deep brown. He kept this from the audience by not turning round throughout the set, which meant that he couldn't adjust the volume on his amplifier. This didn't hide his accident from the other musicians and journalists watching from backstage however, all of whom found the spectacle most amusing.

Fiddle player Dave Swarbrick managed to control his bowels but was so desperate for a piss that he unzipped his fly, stuck his old chap through a hole in the canvas at the back of the stage and relieved himself forthwith. Unfortunately the press area was immediately behind the canvas. "Consequently we've never been popular with Melody Maker since 1970, which I think was the last time they gave us a review," Dave Pegg later lamented to www.folking.com in May 2000.

Tony McPhee's Groundhogs arrived a day late but were squeezed onto the bill, possibly at the expense of Amazing

Blondel, who were there all weekend but never got to play. McPhee recalled being met backstage by Jo Ann Kelly, who told him that none of the acts were going on as they weren't being paid. "I looked out at the soaked audience and, as we have always disliked the playing-pop-star politics that goes on at festivals, we went on not really bothering if we got paid," McPhee later wrote. "It is so unfair on people who have paid for their tickets, forged or not, especially in those conditions, to stare at a stage with nothing going on."

McPhee's altruism is only slightly undercut by Brian Highley's recollection that The Groundhogs had been paid their £100 fee in advance, and that it remained reasonably dry during their set. Playing a typical set of hard-edged, psychedelia-tinged blues rock, the band used photographs of them performing onstage at Krumlin for the rear and gatefold sleeve of their next album, 1971's *Split*. They were appropriate images for an album that fused shamanic blueswailing with a side-long account of psychic disintegration and apocalyptic confusion, as well as containing the band's sole hit single, the pounding but somehow ethereal 'Cherry Red.'

By this time the electric message board was flashing up the infamous message that "Pink Floyd are fogbound in Paris" and would not be appearing that night. As darkness fell, fires were being lit across the site, beacons of unsteady light as anything that could burn was dragged into service in a desperate attempt to keep warm.

Earlier, British blues boom veteran Alexis Korner and his band had agreed to play an extra-long set without being paid. Korner returned, after Fairport had staggered off, to join occultist organ maestro and R&B innovator Graham Bond for another lengthy performance. Bond was at this time at the height of his obsession with Aleister Crowley and black magic; his latest group, the Graham Bond Initiation, had broken up in March, and he had been playing with Ginger Baker's Air Force as well as recording his bizarre solo album, *High Magick* — critically panned at the time, but since regarded as a cult classic.

Alongside Korner, Georgie Fame, Zoot Money and Alan Price, Bond was one of the great British Hammond organ players, straddling the jazz, R&B and rock worlds of the 1960s. Unfortunately as the decade went on he increasingly suffered from mental illness and depression, which was coupled with debilitating drug use and a growing interest in Aleister Crowley-derived occultism. Bond would die falling under a tube train at Finsbury Park station on May 8, 1974, a tragedy generally assumed to be an act of suicide.

Next on were Fotheringay, the band based around lead singer Sandy Denny and her husband, co-vocalist and guitarist Trevor Lucas, who had just released their debut LP. Their second would remain unissued for another 38 years. Sandy had not long left Fairport Convention, following their career-best 1969 album *Liege and Lief*. At Krumlin she was just as drunk as her former bandmates, if not more so: in the event, Brian Highley had to virtually carry the singer on stage.

Supposedly Fotheringay, on learning they weren't getting paid, weren't going to go on, but were drunk and bored enough eventually to do so just for the *craic*. "God, it's really pissing down out there, isn't it?" Sandy reportedly said to the audience. "Sit down, Sandy, you're pissed," replied one of her band. The best-remembered song of the evening was a note-perfect rendition of their album track 'The Sea'. "Do you see the water, and watch it flow?" Sandy sang, as though anyone could miss it (Brian Highley insists that it was still dry when Fotheringay played).

The final act of the night — and, as it turned out, of the festival — was Alan Price and Zoot Money. Price had gone on at about 10pm, just as the full force of the freak storm hit, but kept playing and brought on Zoot as a special guest. Although seeing these two consummate musicians and showboaters, sparring frenetically on their two organs as the storm wreaked havoc around them, must have been quite a sight and sound to behold, it soon became clear that they would be risking life and limb if they continued.

After about half an hour rain started to pour onto the stage, and the drummer erected an umbrella over his kit to stay dry. Price was in the worst danger, playing an electric organ at the front of the stage as water swilled around his feet, poured down onto his head and blew in violently from the hillside. When the main spotlights fused and the stage equipment began throwing out sparks, Brian Highley and stage manager Huw Price made an immediate decision to cancel the show, at least for the night. From a health and safety point of view there was no other choice, even though Manfred Mann Chapter III were waiting to go on immediately after (bassist Steve York remembers soundchecking earlier in the day, to an audience huddled in plastic bags), and The Move had also turned up unexpectedly and were willing to play.

Roy Wood's band would have made a suitable surprise headline act, at least partly making up for the loss of The Kinks, who in turn had been intended as last-minute replacements for The Who. At this point in their career The Move also featured Jeff Lynne, who was already planning (with Wood) the band that would become ELO. But at midnight the music stopped after a series of short circuits to the 2000 watt PA system, and the audience were left to seek out what shelter they could from the fury of the elements.

Most crowded into the large inflatable tent used for the folk concert on Friday evening. Walter Lloyd, who had gone off duty at ten and had "climbed into a sleeping bag in a tent belonging to Ernie, our treasurer," remembers being vaguely aware, though half asleep, that the groups had stopped playing and then that the huge electric fan that kept the tent inflated had also shut off. The tent began to deflate, and Walter heard it flapping violently in the wind, and then a loud crack, "like a whip crack," as it finally collapsed.

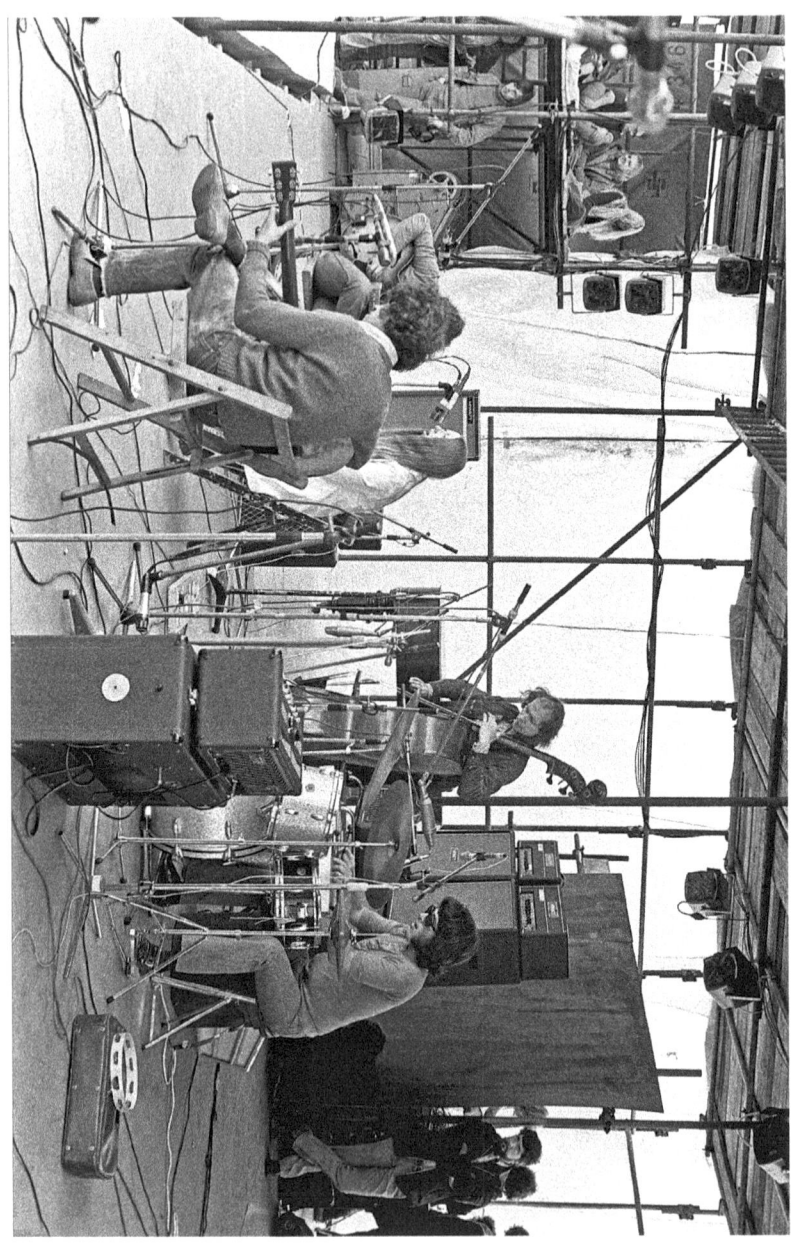

Pentangle

Journey To The End Of The Night

Clive Heenan: "When the storm got really bad, we took shelter in the inflatable Marquee, but the blower broke and it collapsed, nearly engulfing us. We ended up in the pitch black on the moors in torrential rain. We took shelter in a church and a local family opened up an empty house and made a fire so that we could dry out. They invited us round for Sunday dinner. They were very kind. We kept in touch for years.

"I also remember people making a fortune selling bin bags at astronomical prices. People were so desperate to keep dry. I loaned my parka to a girlfriend who buggered off in it. I was left in my leather jacket. I was stained with black dye for about a week as the leather was sopping wet. I'm heading towards 60 now with arthritis in every joint! Ah, foolish youth."

By two in the morning, all Civil Aid volunteers were recalled to duty as the weather was getting worse. Many festival-goers hadn't even brought tents, but by this time it made little difference as almost all the small personal tents had been flattened by the wind. The lucky ones had the large plastic bags that were on sale earlier in the day to protect them from the elements; many had not even them.

The wind and rain was so bad it was impossible even to stand up straight. High on a desolate Pennine hill farm, in the middle of the night and at the mercy of furious storms, teenagers in shorts and sodden t-shirts vainly sought shelter from the horizontal squalls that blasted across the moors like thrown buckets of icy water, by huddling on the lee side of dry stone walls, or attempting to get into the marquee tents that were still standing, from which they were still being driven back by bar staff and security stewards.

The beer tent out front was run by Jack Bunting of the Upper George in Halifax, and just like any pub, the festival marquee had to adhere to strict licensing laws. These were much stricter in 1970 than they are today. Under normal circumstances, Bunting would have risked losing his license if he'd allowed members of the public into the beer tent after last orders at

11pm, and before 11am the next morning. This would have meant losing his pub, which was both his livelihood and his home.

Obviously these were not normal circumstances, but even the Civil Aid report notes that the brewery employees were quite right not to let stray campers into the marquees unless authorised to do so by a higher power. There were also fears of looting and of punters helping themselves to beer throughout the night, but these were secondary concerns.

The indefatigable Ernie decided that hot soup was required, and got the Soyer boiler fired up, chopping up the poles of the collapsed marquee tents for firewood. Walter Lloyd went on a reconnaissance mission to establish what other food supplies were available, and located "four hot dog stands and a milk bar, none cheap." The St John's Ambulance Brigade was already dealing with cases of exposure, so Civil Aid decided "Right. Free soup for all who need it. Keep them warm."

Many campers by this time were so cold they couldn't lift a plastic cup to their mouths, while others were being carried into the makeshift soup kitchens by stretcher. The whole site was on a steep hillside, now a treacherous swamp of mud which could only be negotiated in a downward direction. Yet Civil Aid, St John's Ambulance and Release members did the best they could, carrying warm soup in cups, jars and even the plastic gallon bottles that had previously contained beer and cider, to where shivering masses of young people huddled against the wind and the rain, squatting in the mud outside of the marquee tents that would not allow them shelter.

Eventually, George Graham of Release sent one of the Release doctors to negotiate with the police, and to persuade them that this was an emergency situation and that the beer tents had to be requisitioned immediately to prevent loss of life. By now large numbers of exposure cases were being treated, with as many as possible being transported off site to the nearest hospital by ambulance. According to Civil Aid he managed to get through to the senior officer on duty, and he was persuaded to authorise the sergeant present to open the beer tents (Brian Highley says that landlord Jack Bunting actually arranged this himself).

An officer was placed in each tent to prevent looting, but the Civil Aid report insists that there was not one single case of anyone trying to take a free drink. At first only actual exposure cases were allowed in, but it soon became clear that everyone left outside would become an exposure case if they were not given immediate shelter. There was just enough room for all, and the main beer tent was filled with steam from all the damp bodies pressed together.

Mario Anders was running the bar with Jack Bunting and recounted his memories of the day to the UK Rock Festivals website. "Saturday morning saw a couple of extra loads of beer arrive," he recalled, "I had about five other staff working the tills and serving beer. It was a long day, but thoroughly enjoyable until the weather turned in the mid-afternoon. We carried on serving beer in the rain, but the trade dwindled as the winds began to roar and the rain came in sideways through the front of the tent. We battened down as best we could and two of us stayed inside to weather the storm."

"Sometime in the middle of the evening we got a visit from one of the aid workers asking for me to shelter some people. I was concerned about the risk of theft but we discussed one of us staying up to keep an open eye. I think we had about thirty-five people lying on top of each other but at least we were dry.

"At about 3am I was dozing when I heard an unusual creaking and groaning and woke up to see half of the tent swaying madly in the wind with the pole bending like a twig. We quickly woke everyone under that area, just before the pole lifted off the ground and then slid sideways, snapping some smaller stays and bringing half the tent down. I can still picture the whole thing. Luckily no-one was injured.

"The people were then moved out of the tent. They luckily had managed to get some sleep and were a little stronger. They left, while I stayed. Dawn dragged me awake and I explored outside, to view a scene of utter devastation, but also to see quite a number of people legging it up the field with a slab each under their arm."

Krumlin Mon Amour

Among the items Highley and McEwen had acquired for the festival was an ex-military armoured car which they had parked up backstage, ready to make overnight trips to the night safe of the nearest bank in Halifax with the large quantities of cash they'd expected to take on the gate. Although it was never needed for this purpose, the vehicle did provide a relatively warm and dry sanctuary that Brian Highley could climb into when it all became too much, shutting out the clamour and chaos the festival had descended into.

It was also the location the friendly police officer suggested for a quiet chat in the small hours of Sunday morning. Inside the armoured car, Highley and the constable were joined by the police chief and a doctor, who quietly explained to the dazed promoter that Sunday was going to be very difficult for him, but that a plan of action had already been set in place. He was then administered a combination of drugs apparently intended to both calm him down and keep him awake.

Highley says that he made the decision to cancel the festival at around 4am, after discussions with stage manager Huw Price and the police chief. Apart from the devastation caused by the weather, and the fact that they did not have enough money to pay the bands that were due to appear on Sunday, the stage and electrical equipment had been declared unsafe for use, which settled the matter. Highley adds that the decision was not officially announced until 10am, as if everyone had tried to leave the site at once, in the middle of the night, it could have caused further risks of injury or worse.

With the storm raging overnight and urgent life-saving measures to attend to, it's little wonder that communication broke down between the various parties still trying to run the festival. The Civil Aid team were trying to keep people alive on the campsite and in the main arena; another team was based in the farmhouse; and Brian Highley was trying to hold it together backstage.

Hence, the Civil Aid report states that a meeting of "the new management" at around 6am actually decided to continue with the festival, and that it was only after an inspection of the stage revealed it was in fact unsafe that the decision was made to cancel, at around 8am. Meanwhile, the fact that police told Highley that a plan was already in place suggests that to some extent the matter had been taken out of his hands.

Ultimately, the question of who was in charge by this time and who made the actual decision to cancel the festival is to some extent a moot point. No-one was really in control of the situation anymore, and although by morning the weather had seemingly improved, the main stage was just about the only structure left standing in a scene of utter devastation. Later in the day the weather worsened again, demolishing the few remaining tents and a retaining wall of the farmyard. In short, there was no real possibility of the festival continuing.

As the sun rose the situation out front improved, the bodies wrapped in plastic bags still out in the open came to life, and many began to leave the site. Long queues grew at the soup kitchens, and the second boiler was brought down from the farm to meet demand, but alas at 7 AM even Ernie, the seemingly tireless Civil Aid treasurer, collapsed from the strain. He was taken by a Release doctor to the nearest hospital, together with his daughter Lesley, who was injured when the beer tent had collapsed.

Some fans had taken shelter at the nearby Ebenezer Church, and also the Griffin Hotel, which had stayed open all night to receive refugees. The special festival bus service planned for the close of proceedings in the evening was brought forward to get people off site, and a succession of ambulances crawled onto the site, removing the stoned, the drunk and those suffering from exposure until mid-afternoon.

"Streams of people clutching their clothing to themselves, soaked and freezing, trudged from the field," remembered David Lawrie. Many had to be carried from the mud on modified mountain rescue sledges. Civil Aid teams from Bradford, Leeds and Huddersfield relieved those who had been on duty all night. Walter Lloyd concludes with the following statistics.

"70 extreme exposure cases had been sent to hospital and 330 treated in the first aid tent. It took me about two days to recover physically from Krumlin, and then another three to get some of the loose ends sorted out, especially the financial ones. We were about £200 down overall, including nearly £150 for the Rochdale Unit, whose cheque for the purchase of soup, cups and bread had bounced."

Local young farmers, "fresh from a good night's sleep and no doubt a large fried breakfast," charged £2 to bounce and shove cars out of the mud, while those on foot took the long march into Halifax, long-haired, stoned, bedraggled and covered in mud. Geoff Horan recalls that Halifax was still firmly rooted in the 1950s, but that they found sanctuary in the George: "a good jukebox and like-minded people."

Brian Highley toured the site on Sunday morning, surveying the carnage before announcing the cancellation of the festival at a 10am press conference. Krumlin was now national news, though for all the wrong reasons, having been officially declared a disaster zone. The chief constable read out a statement, while the press kept asking where Derek was, and had he run off with the money?

Highley's final interview of the day was with his old friend and future Labour MP Austin Mitchell, then a presenter on local ITV news show *Calendar*. The interview took place in front of the main stage. When asked where his partner was, Brian finally broke down. "I don't know!" he sobbed on Mitchell's shoulder.

Highley also spoke to *Evening Courier* journalist Gordon Pickles, who had, in happier times, written the festival program. Now he wrote its epitaph. "Standing on the stage on Sunday morning looking out at a flooded auditorium littered with old seats, beer cans and remnants of torn sleeping bags, Mr Highley said 'It's just like a second Hiroshima'."

Pickles (or an enthusiastic sub-editor) ran with Highley's phrase, giving the double-page spread the eyebrow-raising headline 'Just Like A Second Hiroshima'. While it's true that there was rather a lot of litter strewn about the field, one might argue that this was a slight exaggeration, given that no-one had actually dropped an atomic bomb on Krumlin and no-one, let alone several thousand, had actually died (*Friends* magazine reported one death from exposure, but this turned out to be untrue). Highley might be forgiven the comparison, given the strong emotion of the moment, but the *Courier* could be accused of over-egging the pudding, not to mention possibly alarming local residents who had enough to worry about without the fear of suffering radiation poisoning due to the proximity of a failed pop festival (well, who knew what those weirdies got up to?).

The various bands due to play on Sunday were also contacted, either overnight or in the morning, and told not to turn up. Ginger Baker was rehearsing in a hall in Leeds and was told on Sunday morning that bad weather had cancelled the festival. The bands that had played (or turned up to play) gradually departed the site. When their van broke down in the narrow country lane, The Move got stuck.

Pink Floyd had been postponed till Sunday, but Highley had called their people on Saturday night and told them not to bother as he couldn't afford to pay them. This was before the bad weather really set in; ironically, there was a storm clause in the festival's contract with the band, meaning that they wouldn't have to be paid if their set was pulled due to bad weather. But because their appearance had been cancelled before the storm, for other reasons, Northern Entertainments wound up still owing Pink Floyd their £2500 fee. The contract apparently allowed for Pink Floyd turning up a day later than they were booked to play, but not for the promoter to cancel their appearance at the last minute.

During all of this time, Derek McEwen was still missing, his whereabouts unknown. Despite an intensive police search and national news outlets covering the story, this remained the case until five days later. Brian Highley received an apologetic letter from McEwen who said he had walked away from the festival in a state of stress, apparently intending to find somewhere that he could get a couple of hours' sleep before returning to work.

Instead he wandered in a daze on the moors above Scammonden, before hitching a lift with a passing lorry driver to a friend's house in Bradford. From there he headed to Glasgow.

"I was in such a confused state that I just kept on walking and walking," McEwen told the *Courier* on August 27. "It was for about 15 hours right through the worst of the night storm that finally ruined the festival behind me [This was probably not the case, as McEwen walked out on the comparatively calm and dry Friday night]. In the end I reached the home of friends, and I was unconscious there for two days, in a sort of coma. Then I caught a train to Scotland and stayed with more friends, before coming back south."

John Usher worked a ticket booth: "I read later of the missing promoter and the last time I saw him he was at my booth about 5 o'clock checking the cash flow and shaking his head. On asking him how it was going he just slipped me a ten bob note and said cheerio."

In a final coda to the festival, two young American fans got their dates wrong and turned up in Krumlin village a week late. Edmund Desrosiers and Richard Bergerob had travelled all the way from New Hampshire, but found they'd missed all the excitement completely.

After The Flood

Brian Highley and Derek McEwen were both declared bankrupt, though it seems Highley got the worst of it. It transpired that he had been using money from his pub to fund the festival after their backers pulled out. The pub was making less money anyway because he was devoting all his time to organising the event. He left his wife in charge and took on extra staff he couldn't afford: by May he was in serious financial difficulty.

Inevitably Brian Highley lost the Anchor pub in Mill Bank, and also his home. His marriage collapsed and he briefly moved back in with his parents while signing on the dole. All of this was made worse by being in the spotlight of the national media.

After getting a job working for Halifax Rugby League Football Club, Highley went back into the pub trade, managing (but not owning) the Adega in Halifax (formerly the Crown & Anchor) in 1972. Another notable promotion venture involved putting on the legendary US blues duo, Sonny Terry and Brownie McGee, at Halifax Civic Theatre before he moved to the South-West, where Highley managed an ice rink in Bristol and a dance hall in Exeter.

Moving into freelance writing and journalism, Highley contributed to the TV show *Spitting Image* before a chance meeting led to a lucrative career creating new material for the game *Trivial Pursuit*. The first British edition had already come out, but the manufacturers were looking for a team of writers to create a version aimed at kids, ideally made up of a schoolteacher, someone with a track record in comedy, a journalist and someone who knew plenty about pop music.

Highley fulfilled all of these roles and wrote the kids' edition and the baby boomer edition single-handed. He eventually became the sole UK writer for the various updated and specialist editions over the next 25 years. He worked on the unsuccessful follow-up *UBI*, an add-on card set on the theme of entertainment, and became the face of *Trivial Pursuit* in the

UK, as well as its main writer, until his well-earned retirement. Among his last contributions to the game were the *Rolling Stones TP Collector's Edition* and *Classic Rock Trivial Pursuit*, both created solely for the US market.

Derek McEwen re-emerged as an antiquarian bookseller and magazine editor, before dying of cancer in 2002. The Bankruptcy court concluded that "There had been great problems which Mr McEwen and Mr Highley could not possibly control. But there were defects in their administration and a lack of adequate control and supervision. Their organisation fell apart at a time when it was most needed."

The Yorkshire Folk, Blues and Jazz Festival had cost approximately £50,000 to put on. Total income from ticket sales came to just £11,413, accounting for about 5000 of the 25,000 people thought to have attended. The net loss came to £31,431. £4400 was owed to artists, including £2500 to Pink Floyd. The West Yorkshire Police Authority claimed to be owed £2820. An appeal fund was set up after the event, with a couple of benefit gigs at the Grass Roots folk club in Halifax, that succeeded in raising £45 towards costs before the appeal was quietly wound down.

In the 1980s, Banquet House Farm would become known to teenagers of my generation as having the best magic mushrooms in the area, growing not far from where Krumlin's main stage once stood.

Thanks to Brian Highley and John S Wharton; the excellent 'UK rock festivals' website for quotes and much of the initial backstory; Chris Charlesworth and Patrick Humphries for answering my questions; and Andy Greaves, Sam Irvine & all at the Puzzle Hall inn, Sowerby Bridge for support, encouragement and press cuttings.

Dedicated to the memory of Jerry Melanie.

All effort has been made to identify and contact the rights holders of the various photos included, but in many cases this hasn't been possible. Please get in touch if you feel your work has been used without permission.

bleedingcheekpress@gmail.com

Ben Graham, 2020

Lightning Source UK Ltd.
Milton Keynes UK
UKHW020944260820
368848UK00012B/148

Secret Hours